BREATHE

Exchanging Exhaustion
for a Life of Passion

@2013 Traction4Life
ISBN# 978-0-9884904-0-6

Cover Design and Charts by:
Ulhas Moses
www.umsdesign.com

TRACTION4LIFE
P.O. Box 3085
Huntington Beach CA 92605
@traction4life.net

BREATHE

Exchanging Exhaustion
for a Life of Passion

Moses Camacho
with Melinda L Erickson

CONTENTS

DEDICATION

Breathe is dedicated to my amazing, supportive wife, Jill Camacho, and to the family who raised me, and gave me foundation, experience, mentoring—and exercised great patience!

If it were not for you, any of you, I wouldn't be the person I am, the leader God has created me to be. I wouldn't be a man God can use to influence others.

You always stood united, regardless of the challenges we faced. You laid a Christian foundation before me and taught me what a team should look like as we came together to accomplish things that I never could have done by myself, alone.

You have breathed life into me. Thank you for being my NUMBER ONE TEAM!

> "He makes the whole body fit together perfectly. As each part does its own special work, it helps the other parts to grow, so that the whole body is healthy and growing, and full of love."   Ephesians 4:16

"Their responsibility is to equip God's people to do his work and build up the church, the body of Christ." Ephesians 4:12 (NLT)

BREATHE

Have you ever feared that you would be unable to take your next breath? I have.

I remember that day like yesterday. My parents had taken us to the local beach to play in the waves and the sand as we often did as a family. I was 10 that year, and thought I was too old to be playing on the shore, but I was not yet old enough to have the confidence to be out in the deep, facing the dangerous waves.

From the safety of the beach, I watched the surfers and body-boarders swim out to wait for their waves and ride them into shore. It looked easy. They were having a blast, and I had this growing yearning stirring in me to be like them, to experience the rush first hand.

As I watched, I talked myself into being old enough, big enough and skilled enough to surf those waves on my own. I bravely waded out into the water with my board, by myself. It was a lot of work paddling past the breaking waves to the place where I thought the other surfers were catching their waves as they began to form.

Once I got past the white water and into the calm part of the ocean I thought, "That wasn't so bad. I can do this!" The truth was, I really had no clue what I was doing or that I was missing some important information about the nature and timing of waves.

As the next set of swells began to form, I turned around and got ready to ride my first wave. I didn't realize there were going to be six more waves that would follow the first. I started paddling hard to catch it but quickly realized I wasn't deep enough to be at the starting point of the wave. Instead, I was at its breaking point. I was about to experience a wall of water crashing on me instead of having the exhilarating ride I had been expecting.

As the wave collapsed on my back, it threw my board out from underneath me and I found myself spinning underwater, not knowing which way was up or down. I held my breath but started to panic because I couldn't hold it for very long. I remember reaching for the sandy bottom with my feet so I could push myself to the surface, but realizing I couldn't touch, I started swimming. Fortunately, I reached the surface and was able to breathe—for a moment. As soon as I had filled my lungs, another wave came crashing down on me, and I was right back to being under water thinking, "I'm tired, out of breath, underwater, this is it, I'm not going to make it. I'm going to drown!" I fought to come up to the surface again, but just as I gasped for air, the next wave was right there, waiting to plummet me back under. Somehow the tide pushed me close enough to shallow water where I could finally feel the sand beneath my feet and made my way towards shore. How that happened, I don't know, but I was exhausted and relieved to be able to BREATHE again.

Ministry can feel a lot like my experience underwater. Many leaders experience the same overwhelming situation by taking on so much responsibility that they leave themselves no opportunity to BREATHE. The waves of commitment keep coming and we often find ourselves serving as though underwater, gasping for air beneath the surface instead of skimming on the top of the water, breathing in the exhilaration of riding the waves.

Even as a child I remember seeing people who would make a decision to accept Christ, walk a new journey in their relationship with Him, and begin to serve with gratitude, passion and energy—and then find themselves "underwater." Three horrible things can happen to people who feel they are drowning in ministry.

1.   They get tired of fighting to come up to the surface for air, so they decide to get out of the water completely and no longer want to serve in ministry.

2.   Exhausted and gasping for breath, they decide to give up. They no longer want to serve or be a part of a church.

3.   They are so upset with being underwater and not being able to breathe that they walk away from serving and walk away from church. Sometimes they even walk away from God.

Our desire to serve was never intended to drive us to any one of those three decisions. Unfortunately the exhaustion, frustration, and burnout of not being able to breathe and of feeling trapped underwater leads us to make decisions we wouldn't make if we were above the surface, enjoying the waves of ministry.

This book will teach you how to breathe and help you learn how to handle the tides of responsibility in your life so you don't feel like giving up.

You can do greater things through teams. There is no   denying it. We were never intended to do ministry alone. There is no need for breathless exhaustion!

It's interesting, isn't it, that Christ didn't get overwhelmed, burned out or lose interest in helping or serving people. He didn't walk away from ministry, or abandon his purpose or passion. Instead, he managed to build a ministry that outlasted his life on earth—a ministry that is still fluorishing today. How did he accomplish

Christ's goal wasn't to live forever, but to build something that would.

ministry with inexhaustible passion? How did he build a ministry that survived his lifetime? Teams.

Christ's goal wasn't to live forever, but to build something that would.

He modeled working with a team: he chose twelve to share his words with thousands. He poured his life into his team, shared his love, duplicated his compassion, multiplied his desire to meet needs and developed the twelve to work with the multitudes who needed answers to their frustrating, confusing, difficult lives. The result of Jesus' team of twelve is the church we know today. It is the church that still looks out into the communities that surround them and says, "come and see" so that people can have the opportunity to "come and die" to themselves for the sake of their relationship with Christ. When that happens, we see people "come and live" abundant, fulfilled, purposeful lives together.

All this has happened because of the team model Jesus left us. **I think we should pay attention.**

As you lead others using Christ's team model, you make it possible for them and for you to lead through rest versus exhaustion, excitement versus duty and passion versus obligation. Your team members will feel less frustration, have more joy and excitement, more time than tasks: they will embrace their responsibilities, and be equipped to achieve their

> *Without a team, the legacy of your ministry ends with you.*

ministry goals. They will be able to take the time to breathe, to acknowledge God and stand in his presence, dig deeply into his Word and live with his purpose for their lives.

Without a team, the legacy of your ministry ends with you. This book was written to help you accomplish far more in your ministry with a team than you would alone—and leave a legacy that will live beyond your lifetime. Your years on this earth will be a better investment, the results far greater, if you work with teams than if you minister alone.

Teams that begin as relationships and continue as you do life together, in the bond of mentoring and mutual respect, will last. It's not so much about the teams themselves, but about the *relationships* that are created as you work together toward a common goal.

I have learned through success and failure that I can do more for God in the company of others, rather than by myself. I wish I would have learned these lessons earlier, as is always the case when we figure out how to work more effectively. Learning to get more done with less effort, with time to breathe and see the big picture, is a great lesson.

I have lived through moments as a leader that were frustrating and times when I felt isolated and overwhelmed. I often felt guilty because I could not perform to the best of my ability. I knew I could have done a much better job if I would have had more time to work on the project, event, conference, retreat or service. You get the idea; I could have done more, but there was no time to think, or re-organize—or breathe! I was too busy keeping up. If I would have had more help, more people shouldering the responsibility with me, I would have had much more success. I was overworked and felt the shortcomings of attempting success by carrying the load by myself. It is likely that other leaders have experienced these same feelings.

BREATHE is what you are able to do when you develop relationships with volunteers and with teams that have not exhausted you. **R.E.D.** is a method of leadership development I have used with success, and continue to adjust and improve.

> *R.E.D. is all about empowering people to work in teams in a way that prevents burnout.*

R is for Recruiting—relationally! **E** is Equipping—relationally! And **D**—is for duplication. You will duplicate yourself through intentionally nurtured relationships. **R.E.D.** is all about empowering people to work in teams in a way that prevents burnout. It models what Christ did with his twelve. It duplicates YOU! The vision for your ministry, whatever it is, can be spread through more than one voice—through a multitude of stories and illustrations that are carried to the heart of the church where you serve, rather than by you alone. The result is that there is a passion and interest in what you are doing as leaders in the church, and the pervasive belief that it is better to be "here" than anywhere else. What leader wouldn't want that?

"Now as Jesus was walking by the Sea of Galilee, He saw two brothers, Simon who was called Peter, and Andrew his brother, casting a net into the sea; for they were fishermen. And He said to them, "Follow Me, and I will make you fishers of men." Immediately they left their nets and followed Him." Matthew 4:18-22 (NASB)

LEARNING TO BREATHE

I am Moses Camacho. I was the third of six children, born in Corona, California. My siblings and I are all first generation American citizens. We grew up in a low-income neighborhood, but I never realized that as a child. It was just the way things were, and I was a happy, ordinary kid.

BEING FAMILY

My parents met in the strawberry fields. Dad was born into a Christian family with nine brothers and sisters. When they married, he had not yet accepted Christ. Mom was raised in a Catholic home, also with nine brothers and sisters. After their first child was born, Dad's parents invited Mom to church. She was quite open, and gave her life to Christ before her husband. Dad saw major changes in Mom's health and in her life and he began to attend church. Eventually he gave his life to Jesus. His father, my grandfather, was a pastor, so it was natural for my dad to become involved in ministry. As he helped to plant churches, he developed core groups and then moved on. He had the heart of an evangelist, and was inherently a good leader. *He didn't know that he was replicating good leadership and modeling it to the new churches before he left them; he just did it—and all as a volunteer.*

Dad took me with him to the different churches, and when I heard him preach, it held my attention; I was watching him.

My father is the driving force in our family, and is a jokester! Nothing is too serious with him. Mom is the checkpoint, asking questions, making sure everyone is taken care of, guarding the family. Dad is the goofball.

Our family was always supportive. We were very poor with six children to provide for, but there was always enough. I was involved in Little League, city sports and college athletics, and my whole family would be there for games and matches. Even in college they came—and it was a family tradition that was carried on from the time I was about 10 until I was 21 years old. We made it a calendar priority when any of us would perform at something for which we had put in hours of practice. It was viewed as a *family* event, not   an individual event. Even after my elder brother moved to Northern California. The tradition continued. we all still go to watch my nephew play football at least once every year.

> *He didn't know that he was replicating good leadership and modeling it to the new churches before he left them; he just did it—and all as a volunteer.*

That family, team-like commitment carried over into other aspects of our family life, like finances, chores, homework and school projects. I wasn't always excited about being a team in those areas. Yet, for the overall benefit of the family, that close community was integral to our DNA and it worked to keep us committed and gave unity to "our team."

I took for granted my family's closeness, and thought, "All families are this way." But now I know that ours is unique. We WANT to be together. We have an organic love for one another and have fun together. It's like having a big, loud party when we gather. We are passionate, all of us.

MEETING CHRIST

I always knew about Christ, but ultimately made the decision to follow Him and commit the rest of my life to Him when I was 16 years old. I had actually wanted to take that step earlier, but was afraid of a lifelong commitment. I realized that I would make mistakes and felt I needed to be perfect. At a youth camp in the San Bernardino Mountains, the speaker that particular day invited us to accept Christ. He told us that there are ups and downs in life, and we are not always up. He said, "You can choose Christ or you can go through the ups and downs on your own." I responded, "Why not?" I thought, "It's better with Christ than on my own!" I was baptized in my local church down the mountain soon after.

LEARNING TO BREATHE

Dad was always proud of me. He encouraged me in athletics, hobbies, community, high school and college sports. Later

> *"Two people are better off than one, for they can help each other succeed."*
> Ecclesiastes 4:9
> (NLT)

he supported me in my career and ministry choices. He still does. You name it, he is on my side. Did he enjoy it all? No, but he enjoyed his son and I enjoyed my father. That wasn't accidental; it only happened because he was intentional! He left a permanent impression on my life encouraging me to step up to any challenge because I knew that I was not alone.

Problems were always "our" problems. "How do we help?" was the question. The family was always there in pain or suffering, or to celebrate success; they were there when

> *God used my family to teach me that leadership concerns others more than it concerns me.*

career questions came up. All of life's challenges were taken to the family. My family helped me make decisions that kept me on track, and I think that's part of the reason I can NOW rely on a team more than myself. I am stronger with a team than on my own.

God used my family to teach me that leadership concerns others more than it concerns me.

THE PLACE OF CHURCH

Ours was a Spanish-speaking church. It had never been any other way. As a church and as a family, we were always ready to make accommodations to help others feel comfortable in our midst, but no one *ever* would think of attending another church. In our culture, that was unheard of. We would meet the needs of a new person so that there would be no barrier (like using headphones or translating) rather than anyone leaving the church.

As I grew older and was drawn into ministry, I felt a loyalty to the organization in my church, but not the thought process. They had a heart to reach unbelievers, but not in a way that would allow someone from "outside" to penetrate the "church culture" in order to come to Christ. The philosophy was that new people to the church should change to fit in, *rather than being walked through the process of understanding what we believe and how that affects our lives.* The church actually, then, existed more for believers than for unbelievers. Ultimately I had to choose between moving in the direction I wanted to grow in leadership or sticking with my family's church. It was a difficult decision.

Even though in our culture, we *just wouldn't leave,* I did. I had to move on, but it wasn't common and it wasn't easy. I had to follow a new vision and leadership track that they simply couldn't implement and didn't understand.

I felt the sense of separation. It had been the church that brought us together as a family. We all did different things: teaching, business, raising families, but the thing that brought us to the same place every week was church. Breaking tradition and moving into new territory meant we would lose that. If church wouldn't be the thing that brought us all together, then what was it?

We tried to regain our sense of unity in different ways and experimented with having monthly meetings. We rotated homes with one person responsible for the agenda, someone else cooking, someone else planning games. In the end, though, the church was the best way of keeping us together as a family. When we had something to add to the calendar, we were always challenged with consistency.

It takes a partnership, a relationship between the family and a church that is committed. It remains as a core value in my life and in leadership.

Growing up, nothing trumped Sunday church, and as I moved on, it seemed that nothing ever would. Sunday was reserved for God and family. My family had done a good job of instilling that value in us. It made us strong, unified—it was a marriage between our family and giving God glory in our relationships with one another.

In the end, I learned that it was the powerful partnership between family and the church that raised us as kids. Parents have great difficulty raising godly children effectively on their own, and the church can't do it for the parents. *Nothing is as strong as both together. Families need the church, and valuable progress in family issues are difficult to sustain and duplicate without the involvement of the local church.*

It takes a partnership, a relationship between the family and a church that is committed. This remains as a core value in my life and in leadership.

CALL TO MINISTRY.

For a very long time, I didn't know what full time ministry was. When I graduated from high school, my church needed a high school Sunday school teacher for four or five students, so I volunteered. I just developed relationships with the kids, shared God's love and the Word and challenged them to take the next steps in their relationship with Christ. Before long the group started to grow—five, nine, thirteen, seventeen— then the next thing I knew, we had twenty kids in our very confined meeting place. We were out of space. "What else can I do? We CAN'T close the doors," I thought. I asked the pastor if we could meet instead during the week. "Will anyone come?" he wondered. "I don't know. I've never done this before! If you give permission I'll try," I promised. When I told the kids and suggested we meet on Tuesday nights, they thought it would be great to have a youth-focused *service*. We added worship and a message.

After we found more space, more kids came. It was soon out of control. *"What's happening?"* I wondered in amazement. *"What do I do now?* I went to a large church's pastor in the local area to ask if I could meet with the person in charge of their youth. He said, "Oh, our youth pastor?" I thought, "Wow, they have a pastor for young people. That's really cool." When I met with the youth pastor, he told me, "Well, it looks as though you have started a youth ministry." I thought about it a moment. "What?" I answered, "I guess so." *I had no idea what youth ministry was. I was a college student who spent some free time with kids. I had no idea God was developing me into a future pastor.*

The youth pastor coached me and suggested I recruit adult leaders to help. I asked, "What IS a leader?—Why would an adult want to be a part of working with kids?" He helped me understand, and I slowly began working with student leaders until I finally gained enough confidence to ask adults to help. I was afraid to ask people to invest their time with me, mainly because I didn't know what I was doing, so I didn't even know how I needed help! By then I was firmly planted in youth ministry.

At the same time, I was studying at a college in Orange County and wrestling for the school. My goals for education were to be able to have a job that allowed time for family and could provide adequate support. I also wanted to do something that would be enjoyable so I could do this for the long haul. Because I had grown up with a strong family foundation, I knew that providing ample time for my future family was what I would want to duplicate for my own children. I talked with my high school coach who was also an educator and decided to pursue a career in teaching. It seemed to fit all my requirements: financial support, enjoyment and time off to spend with my family. I never would have said I was a youth pastor. I was simply a guy teaching the high school youth class. That's all.

Some of my friends were youth pastors in the area and one summer they invited me to a conference in Washington state called Earthshakers. I took twenty-five kids to the conference where I learned about Oklahoma's *Church on the Move,* and *Church 180* – their youth outreach. After hearing the inspiring stories at the conference, I flew home thinking, "I wonder what God has planned for **me**? I wonder what my story will be? I wonder what direction God will take me?" At that time I was keeping up with the kids, but after the conference I realized that I needed to get *ahead* of them.

I shared the experience and these thoughts with my family. My dad suggested, "God may be calling you to ministry." I understood immediately. He was right.

PREPARATION FOR MORE

I began Bible classes while still attending college, and after college graduation I began teaching. My thought was, "I'll do my career and volunteer in youth ministry."

God had called me for more, but at that time I didn't know how to handle more. Our youth ministry numbers reached 80% of our adult attendance, but this was still a small church organization, and I wondered, "What does more look like?"

I completed the Bible classes, was ordained at 23 and married the love of my life, Jill Heil, when I was 25 years old. We moved to Canyon Lake, found a church that would meet our family needs and began to serve there. The pastor asked me to help with their youth program, since there wasn't one. The program quickly grew from 0 to 60 kids, in a church that had only 100 adults in attendance.

I was being prepared for a larger organization, but I had never been part of one. "Maybe I should look into that," I thought, and discussed the prospect with a youth pastor friend of mine. He had been an accountability partner during my Bible classes, and we had studied together. "Our church is getting ready to do some new things," he told me. "You might want to be a part of this." I wondered how I could stop ministry in my current church, but I believed God was asking me to go. Jill and I loved our current church, the people and the pastor, but if this was God's direction, we needed to follow His lead.

When I resigned and walked into the large organization of my friend's church, I couldn't just sit back and watch. I had to DO something. I volunteered to help my friend with his youth program and started an adult small group with Jill and a couple of friends we had met in our neighborhood.

This was a church with a vision of continuing growth, but the only option for them was to create multi-sites, because the church property was land-locked. I was soon asked to be the youth pastor of the church's first multi-site gathering and was later asked to lead the small group ministry for *all the sites.* This was a much bigger responsibility that would require me to leave my teaching job and accept a role in the church full time.

> *"Commit everything you do to the Lord. Trust in him and he will do this:..."*
> Psalm 37:5 (NIV)

Leave teaching? That had never been a goal. I had never been in full time ministry; I was a public school teacher in Corona. I didn't know if I could do what I was being asked to do full time. Jill and I took a major step of faith and I quit my teaching job to be a full-time pastor - whatever that would mean.

APPLICATION AND DUPLICATION

All of this quickly became the cornerstone for what God was teaching me about leadership. It was developed at the beginning of my life in ministry, but ultimately I believe it was foundational for all that would follow.

I went from not understanding at all what full time ministry was all about to understanding it thoroughly and applying it in all its aspects. I tackled new challenges in ministry and new challenges with my family. I learned about youth, small groups and about multi-site venues. I learned about the value of teams, of relationships and about duplicating volunteers and commitment. I experienced teams that were seriously disfunctional and teams that could breathe and function. Through it all, God had formed in me leadership lessons that I could never have read about in any book. When I made that transition from volunteer leader to full time pastor, I realized that what I had learned along the way about leadership and about duplicating leaders made good, practical sense.

ANOTHER STEP: SADDLEBACK HUNTINGTON BEACH

As God continued to work in my heart, I noticed that I was continually being challenged to leave my comfort zone. I realized that I needed to step into a place that would be less comfortable, where I would have to rely on faith. This place was a new church and unknown territory.

What I know is that accomplishing the Lord's work is more energizing, passionate, sucessful and restful with a team.

My personal leadership goals when I arrived as a new regional campus pastor at Saddleback Huntington Beach were to reach out to the un-churched, and to build leaders. Simple enough goals, though not easy. The lessons I absorbed during those early years of ministry are helping now as I lead on my present church campus. I am learning every day, finding fresh material. **What I know for sure is that accomplishing the Lord's work is more energizing, passionate, successful and restful with a team!**

DUPLICATION TO BREATHE

As I talk with other pastors and leaders and hear their stories and continue to experience leadership challenges myself, I feel an urgency to share the principles that I have learned through my family and through experience with other volunteer leaders who may be wrestling with the same challenges. Developing volunteers who last and don't burn out, who replicate themselves with joy and an understanding of the power of working in teams— who feel significance in what they are doing without burnout is what duplication is all about.

Relationships grown intentionally have allowed me to breathe, to have the time to plan, cast vision and LEAD!

It is all grounded in relationships like the intentional choice my father made with his family, to invest in OUR team as individuals. **Relationships grown intentionally have**

allowed me to breathe—to have the time to plan, cast vision and LEAD! Duplication has been the goal, the ultimate result that has allowed me to keep the circle of responsibility in my life manageable so that I don't feel alone, exhausted and over-extended.

DOING LIFE TOGETHER

INVESTING IN RELATIONSHIPS

The vision of the church will always include a relationship with God and a relationship with people. Because of God's ultimate vision for the church, then, it makes sense that relationships with people run deep as they support the vision of the local church. Those bonds elicit sacrifice for the sake of the relationship. You cannot win your enemies to Christ; only your friends. We love people to the Savior.

> *You cannot win your enemies to Christ; only your friends. We LOVE people to the Savior.*

MENTORING—TOTAL LIFE COMMITMENT

Mentoring, from the beginning of my ministry has been a part of my DNA. There has never been a disconnect between life and ministry—that's how I started in my family growing up, so I didn't know any other way to live as a Christian. It has been a total life commitment.

> *"So now I am giving you a new commandment: Love each other. Just as I have loved you, you should love each other. Your love for one another will prove to the world that you are my disciples."* John 9:23 (NIV)

Matt, Julie and I are very close friends from the last ten years of doing life together. This is the story of my relationship with them. Not that it is such an unusual relationship, but it is an *intentional* one in which we have shared our life's journey together as friends.

About ten years ago, Jill and I bought our home in Canyon Lake, about an hour north of San Diego. We were new to the area and knew no one. Matt was a neighbor behind us, and we became casually acquainted. He was a borderline atheist, at best an agnostic, who said, "Maybe there is a God; I guess somehow the world happened." He would never have believed that Jesus was God or that God has a present role in our lives. He didn't have a firm belief in anything, but believed in possibilities.

One day Jill and I invited Matt and his girlfriend, Julie, to church with us. They were open to coming. The first Sunday we all went out to lunch afterward to continue to build our relationship. We enjoyed each other's company and this soon

Be a good listener. Your ears will never get you in trouble.

Frank Tyger

became a Sunday habit. We would wave during the week and get together on Sunday for church and lunch, but it was just a Sunday relationship. After awhile we took the relationship a little deeper, and began hanging out together outside of Sunday. We started to go out as couples together, having dinner, hanging out as friends *and* sharing our Sundays. We hoped that Matt and Julie would become more open to having a relationship with God.

At this point, we had no deep conversations about God. No intentional "next step," challenges, no asking them "what's changed?" We never discussed whether Jesus was God. We just poured our lives into theirs, listened, earned the right to be a voice in their journey and connected as friends. We even vacationed together.

It was after two years in this growing relationship that Jill and I moved to the large church in another city. We knew we were leaving, but didn't know how to tell Matt and Julie. It was a difficult situation. We wondered how they would respond. We knew they were coming to church because of us. We were friends, we were mentoring them, investing our lives in theirs; we were holding their hands. Now what? We wondered how they would receive the news. We had no clear answer.

One weekend, we planned a trip to Las Vegas to see the shows and hang out together. During the four-hour trip east, we told them our plans. Julie, very sensitive to change in her life, had the most difficulty understanding. "Oh no, what are you doing?" she reacted. "After the first of the year, we need to take this step in a different direction and we will be at a new church," I said, and explained the reasons for the move. "It doesn't make sense!" Julie lamented. We decided to take a gentle approach, knowing how hard it was for them to understand. "We aren't asking you to follow us. We love you and want to keep our relationship; we want to stay together. I just need to learn and grow in areas where this other church organization can help. I am called to ministry, and I am called to grow in leadership." Matt, a businessman, instinctively understood, but Julie said, "Why can't that happen *here*?" They needed time to process this decision.

As leaders, we sometimes want to do what's logical and quick as we respond to the people we lead, but we need to understand who they are as people, and how they process information. Without a two-year relationship with Matt and Julie, we never would have known or understood their reactions. We learned that through having a history of decision-making as friends, problem-solving together and much more. We assured them we wanted to stay together as friends.

In the end, Matt and Julie made the choice to follow us to the new organization. The reason was that church was not the same without their friends. It was the *relationship* that had been built in church, that was *church* to them.

> **THINK ABOUT IT.** *Church programs can "wow" people, but it is far better to walk the journey with them rather than "wow" them with programs.*

Life changed for them as they followed us to the new church. They both accepted Christ. I baptized them together, and I married them in a beautiful ceremony in Maui. We started a small group together. The four of us were the core. Sometimes there were more than that for a while, and then it went back to four. As time went by, I could see Matt changing. He'd say things like, "This wouldn't be possible if there were no God!" They had a difficult time getting pregnant, but we prayed together and eventually having children made the existence of God in their lives very evident.

Matt's vocabulary changed, he prayed in the small group aloud, he was serving in church and choosing curriculum for the small group. It was a whole new Matt!

Tithing was a big step for them. We talked through it because he needed to understand that it was God who was asking, not the church. "But," Matt challenged, "If it's God who is asking, why does He need money?"

It was great to go through all of the questions with him because it allowed

> *"...and how can they believe in him if they have never heard about him? And how can they hear about him unless someone tells them?"*
> Romans 10:14
> (NLT)

me to see God through his fresh eyes! We shared "aha" moments when he understood, as well as those moments when he did not, when things needed to be explained. I had the opportunity to re-experience my own faith through their first-time eyes.

> **STORY:** *Watching Matt and Julie was like watching kids at Christmas, as their faith grew and they experienced new concepts for the first time. I remember one evening, walking with a little two year old boy, Jonathan. On our street, there was one house that had put up what I thought was a measly little eight foot string of "rinky-dink" lights. I was a little irritated that they hadn't put up something better out there. Actually, I thought they were being a little lazy. As Jonathan and I walked that night and we approached the feeble display of lights, he suddenly stopped. I looked at him and his eyes were SO big! "Uncle," he said, pointing, "CHRISTMAS!!!" He was completely enthralled. To him it was a very big deal—an enormous delight! It's the same thing with Christians. So often we simply take the wonders of our faith for granted, and don't value them as a new believer does. In the same way, we often don't understand what value faith has for an unbeliever without a relationship with Christ, maybe because we become self-focused, like I was with that little light string that offended me. I should have been others focused!*

Matt and I sorted through issues about accepting Christ and tried to answer his many questions like, "What does eternity mean?" "How does tithing benefit me and the church?" "How come women are different? Why can't they be more logical?"

We have remained friends, the relationship became stronger and *because of that we have grown closer and closer over the years.* I helped him cross the line of faith, experience church, small group life and marriage. I dedicated their kids. I guess it was natural that they would follow us as God moved us from church to church. Our relationships over the years have grown deeper and closer, as events in our lives have drawn us to that place. We are no longer neighbors or acquaintances, we are lifelong friends through what we have experienced together.

Ours was a relationship you could call mentoring. It is the best way of mentoring I've found—doing life together, bound for the long-haul, committed and forever friends. If I had rushed the relationship, if I'd pointed a finger of accusation, if I'd been anything other than his friend, Matt would have been unlikely to listen. As my friend, in the context of friendship, his life was changed and we will be connected through eternity.

It was the relationship we had together that walked Matt and Julie through the line of faith, from significant relationship with Christ, to dedicating their children, to small groups, to prayer aloud, from 0% to 10% tithing.

When Jill and I moved to the beach cities to take the regional campus pastoral role for Saddleback Church in Huntington Beach, we distanced ourselves out of their reach. In the last ten years, this was our first separation. They have come for the big events in my life, like a special service, special occasion or simply when I needed help. They watch Saddleback services online to stay connected and our friendship remains because it was built on a relationship.

> *"What if I could speak all languages of humans and of angels? If I did not love others, I would be nothing more than a noisy gong or a clanging cymbal. What if I could prophesy and understand all secrets and all knowledge? And what if I had faith that moved mountains? I would be nothing, unless I loved others. What if I gave away all that I owned and let myself be burned alive? I would gain nothing, unless I loved others."*
>
> 1 Corinthians 13:1-3 (CEV)

TIME INVESTED

If all we do is meet and greet on Sunday morning, from the streets to our seats and from our seats to the streets, we are missing the depth only relationships can bring. We need to be patient, which is difficult for church leaders. We tend to want overnight growth. The goal of the church is not overnight growth; it is to bring people to Christ. Our goal isn't a better church for the people who are attending; it is to be a better church for the un-churched to go to. Like with Matt's story, it takes time. Walls need to be broken down, hurt repaired, damage healed. It's a process of life-change that we walk through. That is why we need to walk alongside people in relationships!

MATT'S STORY: *"I had just been through a break up of a long time relationship and I was hurting. Julie, who later became my wife, was my friend and thought I should meet this friend of hers, Moses. 'No,' I told her. 'I don't need to meet him.' I wasn't closed-minded or anything, I just didn't see how meeting this Moses guy could help. Later, Julie asked again and I agreed to meet him. We developed a good friendship. He took me to meet his family and I felt like I became part of it. That crazy Moses got us going in our spiritual lives. When Moses and Jill moved to another church, we didn't understand, but we followed them and super-enjoyed the move. We began serving and hosted small groups. I kept growing and learning how to be the man in my home and a lot more.*

How did that make a difference in my life? It was the impact of Moses' invitation to be a part of his life, to be a friend and have a relationship together that made the difference in mine. He invested in our lives and he taught us a step at a time how to be followers of Christ. From tithing to baptism, even if I didn't completely understand as I do now, I did it anyway. Without Moses reaching out to me, caring, wanting a relationship with me, my life would be much different.

He is still involved in my life. Sometimes when Julie and I are at a crisis point in our marriage or just need good advice, one of us says, 'we should talk to Moses about that.'

I can't believe I've gone from that place of saying, 'I don't need to meet him,' to what we have now. It's the same with God. People do need to meet him, they just don't know it. Look how he has changed our lives. We have invited so many people to come to church with us, and we have invested in so many others. I'm kind of a shy guy, but we invite people even though we don't know what will happen. We don't know what God will do!"

THINK ABOUT IT: *The depth of a relationship overcomes the uncertainty associated with change. People always struggle with change, but what helps in those changes is the relationship that you have developed together. You trust that relationship and each other more than the uncertainty that overwhelms you. For example, Julie struggled with change as she was growing up. Nothing was constant in her life as a child, and as an adult, she continued to carry that struggle. However, as* *an adult in a caring mutual relationship such as our two couples had together, the consistency of that relationship overcame the uncertainty of change. When I moved in my own role at church from a Sunday morning live service to a Saturday night launch, then to a satellite, then to a new campus, it was not the vision of the church that kept moving them, it was **the relationship** we had together as they followed us through all those moves.*

Recently, Matt and Julie have begun to attend a church that they chose themselves, as their "own" church. "The weird part of this church," Matt said, "is that you're not included." Now they are making decisions based on what they learned from Jill and me over the course of our relationship, and based on what is best for their family. Matt doesn't have any desire to do ministry as a career. He is a business owner who now has a desire to be used by God and to see his church be successful. He has a huge concern for his pastor, a concern that would probably never have been there if not for the relationship we had together. Ten years allows a great depth of understanding and love.

THINK ABOUT IT: *If the church isn't growing, the first question we need to ask is whether we are serving the people and meeting the needs of the non-church attenders.*

Is the service structured in a way that people who are un-churched feel welcome, wanted and valued? If the answer is yes, the next question to ask is whether the members are being taught to build relationships with unreached people.

LIFE AND MINISTRY

I have never separated my life and ministry. It's more about how my life tells a story to others rather than preparing to teach them with a book and content.

My life "stories" speak to my children, and to everyone around me, including the leaders in our church. My boys learn more from watching me than my telling them, and from making their own choices than they learn from being told. It's important as a leader that I be an example worth following.

STORY: *I read books all the time, but when I pull out the Bible, my three year old twins know that the Bible is different, somehow. These little boys know from watching me and spending time with me, what things are of God. They are learning the difference between what is God made and what is man made. They know the difference between the Bible and another book. They know that from our time together and the conversations that we have. I ask them a question, and then they learn and absorb my life story amazingly well.*

Your life will be the greatest witness through relationships. Life without relationships is nowhere near as impactful as life with relationships. The same goes for ministry and for growing healthy, intentionally relational teams that learn to breathe in sync.

RELATIONAL PERSPECTIVE

I have read dozens of leadership books and attended all the seminars I could fit into my always overcrowded schedule, but it seemed as though I could find no book or person who could tell me where to start, how to begin leading my leaders. Fortunately I have had great relationships with leaders in my life who allowed me to tap into their knowledge and expertise. Much of it was learned from my family and as a volunteer—all of it rested upon the foundation of relationships.

> God will take you through successes and failures to allow you to stretch in all the areas of your life.

The chapters that follow represent what has actually been put into practice, and what is a part of real-life ministry. It is written from the perspective of my experience of success and failure in the past, but also with the vantage point of the present.

RECRUITING

RELATIONAL VS. NON-RELATIONAL

Here is where we began. A series of ministry leader's meetings unfolded all that I hoped would be helpful, all that I believed God had shown me to be successful in casting vision and reproducing leaders who would reproduce teams, and ultimately find success.

All great churches focus on three things:

1. Reaching out to the unreached, to those who are not connected to Christ or a local church.

2. Building up their members to be disciples (followers of Christ).

3. Sending them out to repeat the process in others.

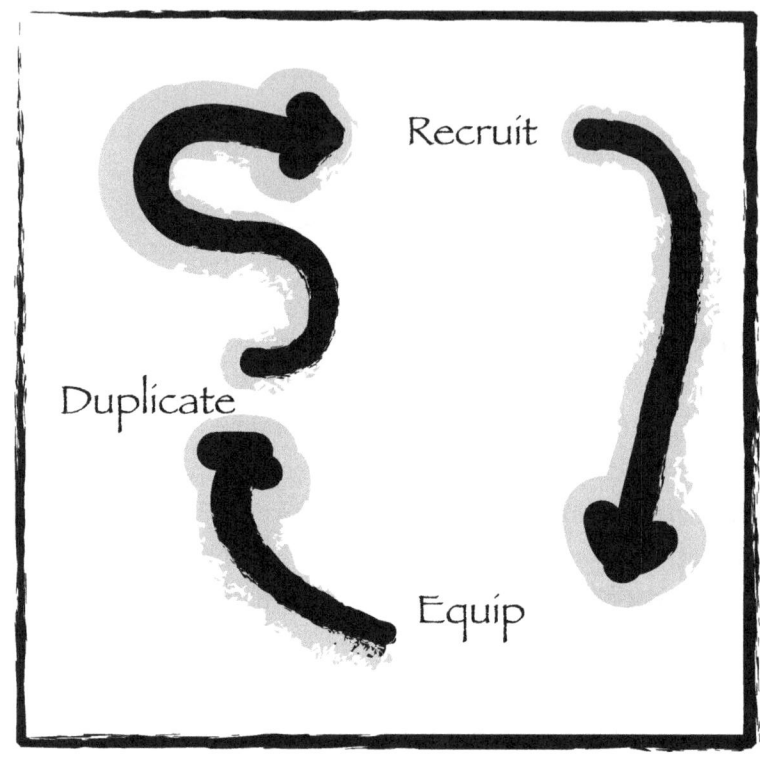

I call the process of accomplishing these three things **R.E.D.**, an easy acronym for:

R ecruiting
E quipping
D uplicating

There are two ways to do this in the church:

Relationally	Non-Relationally
Personal relationship	Banners
Personal invitation	Billboards
Personal mentoring	Fliers
	Newsletters
	Newspapers
	Social Media
	Website
	Stage Announcements

Both of these methods can be successful, and they comprise several different ways of accomplishing the goal of getting people to church. People who are already seeking will be attracted by the website, social media, signs, etc. They are the people who have just moved into the area and are looking for a church home. They know where to look, how to discern what place is the best fit, and how to connect. However, for people like Matt who would in no way come to church through a non-relational tool, we may be missing the mark. Matt had driven by dozens of churches, seen multiple creative fliers, had several tracts put on his car and doorstep, but the truth is that none of those tools worked. It wasn't for lack of advertising from the church, it was a lack of investment in his life.

What affected life change in Matt was someone investing into his life first, and then walking alongside him. He saw no value in church or in having a relationship with God. He was not attracted to church because of its fine facility or location, or a banner or flier. *He simply would not go.* The only way for someone who is totally unconnected to Christ to connect is through a committed personal relationship. It requires someone who has personally built a caring friendship with him, explained what a relationship with Christ is, and what benefit it holds for him. Without that kind of relationship, the only imprint they have of a Christian is what they have been exposed to in the public domain, and that is not always positive.

THREE STORIES: *In high school I brought my unchurched friend Brian to church with me and sat him down in the front row. It was a charismatic church and the pastor was preaching with energy, fire and brimstone. For me, this was common, a normal Sunday worship experience. Midway through the service, Brian leaned over and whispered to me, "Why is he so mad?" It caught me off guard, and I was trying to understand his question. I answered him in my best Christianese, "That's the Spirit, brother. The influence of the Holy Ghost!" He answered me in his best unchurched language, "I don't get it." I had no further answer for him. "Just listen," I told him.*

I took Jason and another friend with me to a different church, one that ours had partnered with. I thought they spoke the language of the unchurched a little better, but it soon became evident that this church wasn't meeting their needs either. Jason asked, "What's going on?" I didn't understand. "What do you mean?" I asked. "Why are they dancing around?" "They are in the spirit," I answered. "What?" Jason said. "It looks like they are aware of what they are doing to me." I had no more answers. "Just watch and listen," I told them.

A revival service was in full swing, and the power of the Holy Spirit was taking over. I thought, "The power of the Holy Spirit will explain things for me. The evangelist was speaking about the miracles of God, and how he can break walls, loosen chains. He exclaimed, "Pray you will be free!" People were being slain in the spirit, dropping like flies. My friend, Ray, was scared to death. "What's going on?" he asked; it was the same question Jason had posed. I should have gotten it. The evangelist asked him to come forward. Ray answered, "No!" The evangelist persisted, "Come on up here," he said. My mind was racing in those moments, lost in the evangelist's message to Ray. "This is it," I thought. "This is the story I will share about life change in my friend Ray because of this spirit-filled service." It would happen, I knew it would. The life change, the story that I dreamed would be used to motivate others to bring unchurched friends to Christ was about to happen. My imagination was soaring. I would recount it as the moment that I brought my friend who didn't have a relationship with Christ and the evangelist who was used to break through to him. Ray would be changed forever from being a guy who didn't have an eternity secured with God, didn't have direction, didn't know his gifts let alone put them to use." I looked up and waited to see what happened next. But, the words that came out of Ray's mouth were, "No, thank you." Oh no! My hopes were dashed. What happened? "What more could I have done to orchestrate this?" I wondered. "Where did I go wrong? This can't be right!"

The church I had grown up in was not connecting with people who were unchurched! They were unwilling to relate to people as they were, understand their culture and do life with them.

These experiences showed me how important it was to be certain that I was connecting with the unconnected in a way that they could understand. It had been a painful, disappointing lesson, but well worth learning. Relationships were the way to go!

"I want lovingkindness and not a gift to be given in worship. I want people to know God instead of giving burnt gifts." Hosea 6:6 (NLV)

R.E.D.

RECRUITING
FROM THE COMMUNITY

We are a bridge for the community to come to Christ. We are not just signs in the parking lot. We start with introducing people to the weekend experience, help them to develop relationships with US and ultimately with Christ. In our church we have a process for people to meet Christ and mature in their spiritual journey, but we are also engaged in walking with them throughout their lives. Recruiting takes people from the darkness of the streets to a relationship with Christ—and from their first day as a new believer, to become ready to serve. That can happen very quickly or require much love and patience.

STORY: *Julie accepted Christ after years in a caring relationship with Jill and me. "Church has done so many amazing things in my life," Julie said. "It has taught me to forgive others and to forgive myself. Church has given me the most amazing friends and church family. It was at church that I learned life lessons and received guidance for my life. People have been my support system at weekly services and in small groups. They have been our friends." Because of her relationships within the church, and with Jill and me, Julie is committed to connecting others to the same benefits she has experienced. "I have seen what God has done in my life and the lives of my children and husband. I invite my friends, family and others to church because I believe we all deserve the best... we all need to plant seeds with people in our lives and pray that they choose to water those seeds. Sometimes it takes a lot of planting, but the return is unbelieveable!"*

SERVING THE COMMUNITY

Our "community" includes a population of more than 600,000 including adjacent cities. Statistics reveal that nearly one in five Americans say they are atheist, agnostic or "nothing in paricular." Less than 50% are Protestant. (Pew Forum on Religion and Public Life, October 2012) In addition, a 2009 Gallup Poll states that 45% of Protestants claim that they attend church on a regular basis. If we are the norm, that would be 465,000 people who are not connected to a local body of Christ that is helping them to grow spiritually; they have no one to walk alongside them through their life's journey.

As a church, we want to move out of our comfort zone and *decrease that number!* That will only come through individual relationships, by personally taking responsibility and focusing on people in the community who are not yet connected.

> *"But Moses said to God, 'Who am I that should go to Pharoah, and that I should bring the sons of Israel out of Egypt?' And He said, 'Certainly I will be with you...'"*
> Exodus 3:11-12a (NASB)

I've never read about or seen anyone do anything great by being comfortable. Think of Noah, Moses, Jesus or the apostle Paul. They all went through awkward moments of refinement. We need to intentionally create conversations. It might be awkward, but it may also be refining.

At our church one year we used graphics, blogs, illustrations, success stories and wristband reminders that said, "Connecting the Unconnected" to help us remember the vision amid the busyness of life. All were geared around connecting our unconnected community to Christ. We walk by hundreds of unconnected people on a daily basis, so whenever we come together we need to be reminded of our responsibility, and that it's important. The community doesn't know Christ. Thousands in our community have no idea what a relationship with Christ is, but *we know.*

BUILDING PEOPLE

We need to focus on building relationships with people. A healthy church reaches out to the community, it builds people up and then sends them out to do the same thing. As that happens, our team becomes sronger and our leaders are better able to breathe.

Every church that is engaged in changing lives is doing this. Once a new believer's questions are answered, the church sends them out to reach others. ***How that happens is very important.***

> **THINK ABOUT IT**: *The ultimate priority of our lives is loving God and loving others. Loving people doesn't happen through advertisements, it happens through conversations and time spent with each other. Are we loving people? "So now I am giving you a new commandment: love each other. Just as I have loved you, you should love each other. Your love for one another will prove to the world that you are my disciples."* John 13:34-35 (NLT)

I have a habit of not being in the office, but being in the community as much as possible. I want to connect with the community we serve and the people who live and work here, and intentionally build relationships with those who are not acqainted with Christ. All my staff meetings and one on one meetings are in the community we are trying to reach. Putting myself in the middle of the people I am trying to engage will ultimately help me connect with them, understand how they think, how they talk, what's important to them and what's not. I wouldn't learn any of that inside an office or conference room.

STORY: *It was a regular workday, and I had a number of meetings scheduled, so I arrived in the coffee shop early and walked up to the counter. "I have quite a few meetings today, Jess, and I wonder if you would mind if I used the table over there," I gestured toward the window. "No problem," the tattooed server answered. "Are you going to buy anything?" he asked. I smiled. "I don't want to just take up space. Of course we will contribute to your business." Jess was curious. "What are you doing here?" I answered, "I am a pastor in the area and will be meeting with people throughout the day." Jess understood. "Church stuff," he said. I smiled again. "Yeah, church stuff." Jess wanted to continue the conversation. "There used to be some people who sat at that same table. They came in early, read their Bibles and other books, talked and then left. I never understood them." I asked Jess what he meant. "I didn't get a good vibe from them," he explained. "They came in and ordered drinks, but they looked at me and my tattoos. I felt as though I was being scrutinized.*

The way they looked at me made me feel as though they thought I was less of a person than they were." Jess continued, "I didn't understand. They were reading the Bible. I assumed that reading the Bible would make you a better person. But they judged me, took up space, made a mess and walked out. I was confused."

As Jess spoke, and I heard his experience with church people, my heart was heavy. Here was a scenario where a young man didn't have a relationship with God and had no Christian in his life. Here was the perfect opportunity to connect and relate with Jess, to help him move closer to the greatest relationship he would ever have. Yet, "church" people who had that precious relationship had driven him further away instead of closer. I felt compelled to apologize on behalf of these church people. "I'm sorry they made you feel that way, and I'm even more sorry for how their behavior interprets Christian life. I can't change what they did, I don't know them, but I hope I can give you a better image of Christians." Jess was kind. "Oh, no worries. I understand it's not your fault. I was just confused because I saw them reading and talking about the Bible, but I never did see any change in them—or even any action from what they were reading and discussing."

I've been back numerous times to continue my relationship with Jess, and I'm on a first name basis with the owner of the coffee shop and the workers. Maybe Jess isn't much closer to giving his life to Christ, but I think I have played a role in getting him from maybe a -10 to a -9 in his view of Christians and being open to wanting to know more. It was, perhaps, his "next step" in moving toward Christ.

Our goal is to bring people from the community to be a part of the church body. We were never intended to be alone in our lives, without a church family. We need to be a bridge to bring people in, connect, be family, and develop intimate, caring relationships with one another. As the body of Christ, we are a tangible representation of God—every day.

WINNING THE COMMUNITY

Every church has a vision. That vision is tied to how we identify ourselves in the community. We are always asking the question, what will drive attention to us? We have a rather famous "mother" church, because Rick Warren is well-known. But our goal isn't to attract the people who already know us because of our identity with Saddleback Church. We want our audience to be people who don't know who Rick Warren is, who have never been connected to a church at all. We want to be a premier place for families in our area, for college students, for adults and for children. We want to be known in the community as a place where people can find answers to all of their problems, where they can fill the spiritual void in their lives, where they can discover their purpose, get help with parenting and much more—*because we are all doing life together.* Bottom line: we want to connect those who are unconnected to Christ by being a church filled with care and love.

There are relational and non-relational ways that we connect with the community.

Non-relationally, we provide *THINGS*:
   Signs at the church
   Flags on the streets
   Street arrow twirlers
   Yard signs at members' homes
   Postcards
   Banners
   License plate frames
   Website
   Social media
   Newspaper ads
   Fliers
   Invite cards

On the relational side, we provide OURSELVES, reaching out to:
   Neighbors
   Community members through events and service projects
   Co-workers
   Family members
   Small groups

Our choice is to be RELATIONALLY driven because it is through relationships that we have the highest possibility of success in inspiring someone to make a decision for Christ, to take a step of faith and then sustain that commitment. Not that non-relational methods of touching our community aren't helpful. Even non-relational methods can be made more relational if they are given that spin.

For example, our website is filled with blogs that talk about how much we love our community, about projects, events, attitudes, sermons and about people with caring hearts. That relates the message that our church is interested in people, cares for the community and is doing something about it— relationally.

On the flip side, our traffic ministry is highly relational. It has two focuses. *The first focus is making a good impression on our visitors.* Volunteers stand at the entrances to our parking lot and smile and wave to the people in our community who drive by on the street. It doesn't sound or look like an exciting ministry to be a part of, nor on the surface does it seem as though it would be an important part of our service. They just put on their fluorescent vests and stand out there, smile and wave. However, first impressions are important, and our traffic greeters make that first impression of our church.

> *The signs tell the community we are here, but the people show them that we care.*

They are the first people visitors see when they drive into the parking lot.

The second focus of the traffic ministry is the *people in our community who have already made the decision to NOT go to church. But then, they see that friendly wave* on a Sunday morning and have the opportunity to connect. Over and over again I hear first time guests say, "I kept seeing those people out there waving. I drove by several times but didn't know the church was there until I saw someone waving. I thought, 'this place is unique,' so I decided to check it out."

Should we leave it to the signs? Probably not. *The signs tell the community we are here, but the people show them that we care.* People in our traffic ministry LOVE it. It's a chance to engage in a relaxing, comfortable way by simply waving to people. Theirs is a small effort that brings a big return. We plan to do more to make this a spiritual moment for our traffic team, to teach them to pray for the people as they drive by, and to realize that they are standing there on the curbside between frustrated, stressful lives and the opportunity to exist with direction, purpose, spiritual and emotional health.

> *"And the master said to the slave, 'Go out into the highways and along the hedges, and compel them to come in, so that my house may be filled.'"* Luke 14:23 (NASB)

BUILDING PERSONAL RELATIONSHIPS

We are on a journey toward spiritual growth together with the teams we relate to, and with the teams we are yet to recruit—a journey toward spiritual growth. Our goal as a church is to take people with no connection with Christ on a journey that will bring life to their new faith and deepen it, taking them from "come and see" to "come and die"—so they can live a life of purpose, direction, joy and peace. WE as leaders and church members relationally provide "come and see" opportunities for people we meet.

The chart on pages 70-71 reflects the process of leading the community through spiritual growth and involvement, to ultimately live a life that is duplicated in others. It all starts with relationships in the community.

BREATHE

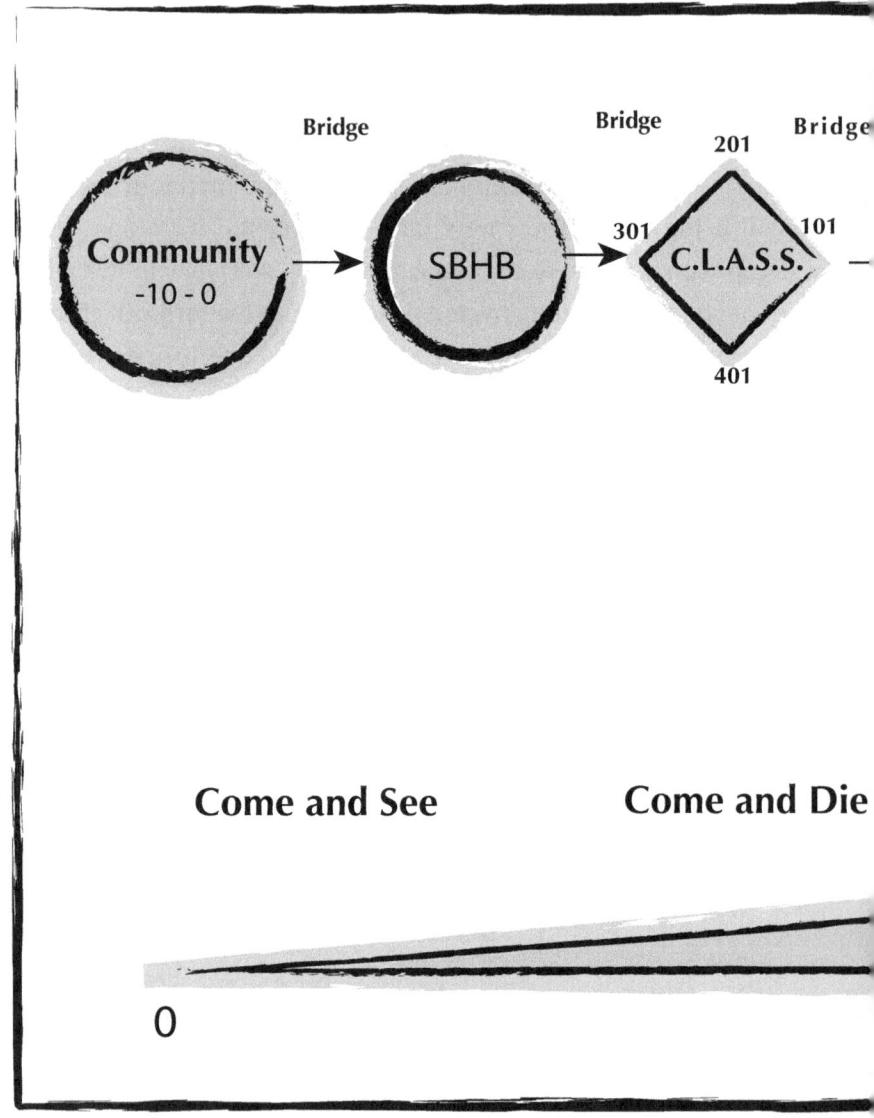

70

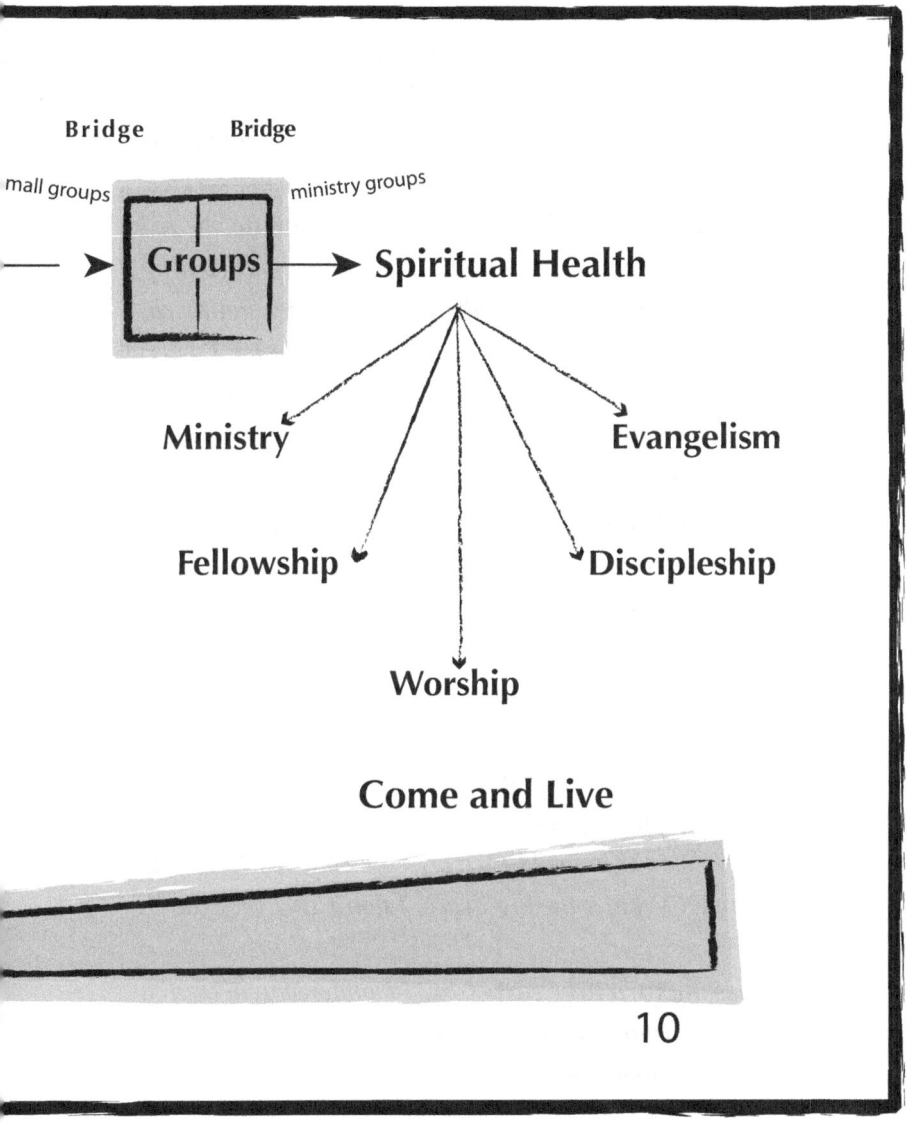

STORY: *I have recently been playing basketball with some un-connected guys who were definitely not in the habit of church. Not at all. But I had been spending time with them, developing a relationship with them, and I was excited and ready to ask them to come to an Easter service. I had thought, "Here's an opportunity to invite them." Rather than saying, "why don't you think about coming to Easter service?" I decided to take a bolder approach, assuming that they WERE going somewhere for Easter. "Its Easter after all! Everyone goes to church on Easter," I reasoned. Of course, this wouldn't be the approach I would take if we didn't have a relationship. But we DID and I had relational equity in their lives. I was certain that I could be more honest and direct with them than I would be with someone who was simply an acquaintence. So, I prayed and mustered up my courage and asked Alex the question, "Where are you going to church for Easter?" The answer came back, "I'm not going." I asked, kind of joking around, "Not going! How can you not be going? It's Easter, man!" I said. "Even athiests go to church on Easter." Alex was visibly surprised at my reaction. He wondered, "What's the big deal? I don't DO the church thing."*

It was my turn to be surprised. I wondered why church wasn't important to this young man. The opportunity was open for more spiritual conversation, but the bottom line was that he didn't think that church had anything to offer him.

After the wall broke down, and the thought of the possibility of going to church on Easter was broached, the first question he asked was not what cool videos we had, who was speaking, who the band was, whether the music style was young or old or whether we offered skits or light shows. He didn't care if we offered donuts or a children's program, whether the youth ministry rocked, or even if we had comfortable seats, great signs or bulletins. Those are the things that many churches, including ours, spend several hours and several dollars working hard to get right. Instead, the first question on his mind was, "How long is the service…?"

Easter arrived, but he didn't come to the 9 a.m. service, so I sent him a text saying he'd missed the early service. "But the 11 is coming up!" Alex wrote back and said, "You sure are persistent! I've got to hand it to you for giving it a shot." I texted back, "It was worth a try." Then I followed up with another, "Correction...YOU were worth a try!"

It's important for us to have these kinds of relationships because church is not important to the unchurched. There are more than 465,000 un-connected people in our area of influence who see no value in a relationship with Christ. It's our responsibility then, to be a bridge to their hearts, to help them want to "come and see" what a relationship with Jesus is about, and from our lives, why they should commit to Him too. They need to know why church is important, why God is important, and why they should change their Sunday schedule to fit church into their calendar.

> **THINK ABOUT IT.** *I have noticed that the further a person is in the process of spiritual health, the further they may be from the evangelism pool. We need to work to reverse that, to think like visitors, unbelievers, not from our Christian mindset. We need to do church "with" people, as I did with Matt and Julie, not "to" them, and be sensitive to where they are in their journey.*

DISCIPLESHIP - BEYOND THE FRONT DOOR

The weekend is only the beginning of engaging the community. All that is needed in our lives can't happen there.

Small groups are not just a good idea, they are God's idea. We often have a short window of conversation with people on Sundays; there is no time or opportunity to develop relationships. Small groups take us to a deeper level with the community, and are a place to be heard and to share. It is a time to allow others into our lives. **A small group is a team.** A healthy church will reach into the community to bring people to faith and spiritual maturity and then turn them back into the community to reach others. **Small groups are important**

players in that journey toward the spiritual health of the church.

> STORY: *Jessica had been attending our church for about a year, and one summer she felt a strong desire to take our basic discipleship C.L.A.S.S. 101 for all the "normal" reasons. She wanted to learn as much as she could about our church through this introductory class. She wanted to know how to have a better relationship with Christ, and she also wondered how she could be used to help others know him. She DID learn a lot about our church. "But," she said, "I also received a bonus! The bonus was the number of great relationships God gave my family because of our involvements with C.L.A.S.S. 101 AND an incredible **small group**." When Jessica and her husband went to the C.L.A.S.S., they weren't looking for a small group. They knew they needed one, but had some concerns because of their young child. "At the end of class, Joe and Sarah from across our table told us they were opening up a small group." As they described it, Jessica knew it was perfect for them. "Now that we have been together for awhile, I believe God put all of us in that 101 class so we could become a small group FAMILY!"*

The purpose of relatiaonships is to grow spiritually. We need to constantly evaluate the spiritual health of our church, and it is how we engage people and walk them through the process of spiritual growth that is critical. *It is the place of teams to bring that about—to be able to breathe and enjoy the journey together. As that occurs, the church will become stronger and be better able to breathe collectively.*

> *"There are different kinds of spiritual gifts, but the same Spirit gives them. There are different ways of serving, but the same Lord is served. There are different abilities to perform service, but the same God gives ability to all for their particular service. The Spirit's presence is shown in some way in each person, for the good of all."*
>
> 1 Corinthians 12:4-7 (GNT)

R.E.D.
RECRUITING
VOLUNTEERS AND LEADERS

> *"Come to me, all you who are struggling hard and carrying heavy loads, and I will give you rest. Put on my yoke, and learn from me. I'm gentle and humble. And you will find rest for yourselves. My yoke is easy to bear, and my burden is light.* Matthew 11:28-30 (CEB)

Often I have seen people transition from living life without Christ, then come to Christ, get baptized and have this burning desire to be used by God. It's exciting and it's all good! The not so great part is when I see people step in and start serving (volunteering) in a ministry or several ministries, and before long, they are unable to breathe; they are overwhelmed, frustrated or angry. What happens next is not good, and it happens too often.

One of three things occur when an overwhelmed volunteer-steps away from their relationship with Christ:

1. **They leave ministry.**

They step up to so much responsibility that they don't know what to do with it all, so they ultimately get burned out and step down from serving/volunteering and are left with a negative perspective toward ministry.

2. **They leave ministry and church.**

They have such a bad experience that they not only step down from ministry but they step out of the church in general.

3. **They walk away from ministry, church and God!**

> *If you don't have peace, it's not because someone took it from you. You gave it away.*

In any of these cases the new believer is angry at the church, angry at the staff, angry at the leaders and sometimes even angry at God.

What happened? How did someone move from energy, excitement and passion to suffocating burnout, frustration and anger? They had NO TEAM: ministry happened without Christ's model.

JESUS RECRUITED TO DUPLICATE

Out of all the world leaders from the beginning of time, there has never been a man who has done what Jesus did! No religious leader, no government leader, no business leader, no non-profit leader has ever had the impact that Jesus did. I will tell you why. Consider these names, Buddha, Gandhi, George Washington, Abraham Lincoln, Warren Buffet, Donald Trump. Who can name the people on their teams? Okay, name the *three* people who worked closely alongside them. Other than a historian, very few of us could remember if these leaders even HAD a team, let alone name them.

One of the major things Jesus is known for is his team of twelve disciples. He personally recruited those twelve and spent three years equipping them. These are the men he left behind to carry on the work of ministry so that what Jesus began in the world would continue.

> "I've given them the glory that you gave me so that they can be one just as we are one." John 17:22 (CEV)

He grew a ministry that would outlast his life on earth. What better way to build a team than to pour his life into theirs and duplicate himself? It was effective. More than 2,000 years later, here we are, doing as a church what Christ started through a team of twelve. He passed on his time, his gifts, his love, his encouraging words, his lifestyle model and his heart for God. "I've given them the glory...," he said. He was always about others, never about himself. His life was all about relationships.

If you're not influencing people, then you're not leading them either.

CREATING TEAMS THAT BREATHE

When I arrived in Huntington Beach, we had a team of great volunteers. They had been there for nine months since the campus had been in existence, and I was careful to encourage and appreciate them regularly.

After nine months, they were still excited, but burnout was around the corner if I didn't help them learn to recruit relationally to build a team. Recruiting was a key piece in the team puzzle. Because recruiting more volunteers was perceived as the need of the hour, the ultimate goal was reaching out to the potential volunteers and leaders in the church who were not already serving.

I presented this simple chart (page 83), which the volunteer leaders could all easily relate to. When a team is small (maybe just you) and the responsibilities are huge, the leader's passion and that of the volunteer go down, along with their creativity. They are headed for burnout.

On the other hand, when the team is larger than you or your responsibilities, everyone benefits. The team is always anxious to do more, you are full of passion and creativity, and the responsibilities are accomplished well, to the best of everyone's ability.

The importance of growing a team is so that as the ministry becomes long term, a team is in place so the vision continues to be implemented without you. That is what Christ did: he built his team to build the church that is still fluorishing today.

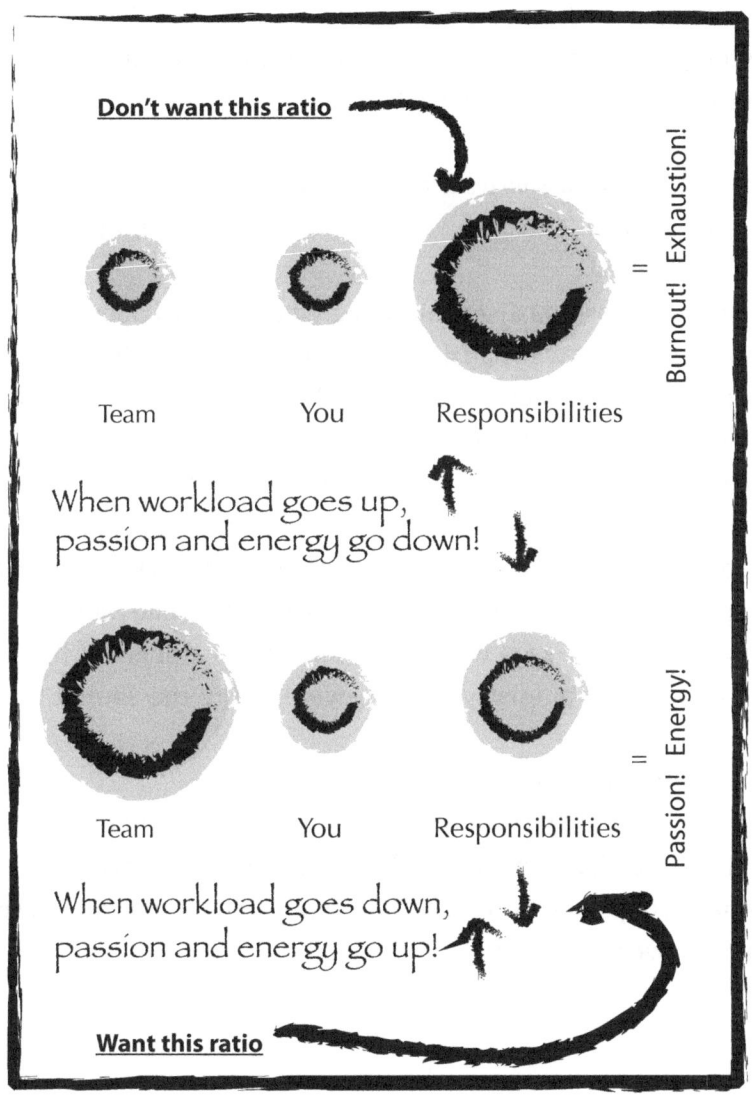

Don't want this ratio

Team   You   Responsibilities   = Burnout! Exhaustion!

When workload goes up, passion and energy go down!

Team   You   Responsibilities   = Passion! Energy!

When workload goes down, passion and energy go up!

Want this ratio

Doing ministry alone is a sure way to run out of breath. The alternative that will allow you to breathe and see ministry last for the long term is having a team.

> *"Iron is made sharp with iron, and one man is made sharp by a friend."*   Proverbs 27:17

It was enormously encouraging when I heard about a new ministry leader who had drawn the three circles during her first "official" team meeting. She erased them two or three times to get the sizes right and explained to her team, "We need to have a large enough leadership team so that the responsibilities don't overwhelm us. We need our responsibilities to be a reasonable, do-able size." The exciting thing was that she was replicating what she had heard from a leader I had taught, *not from me*, and passed it along to her team members. I hoped that the other ministry leaders were doing the same thing.

YOU OR TEAMS?

At one meeting, I asked the ministry leaders to call out all the things that happen in the church, from Sunday worship to small groups and outreach. The list I placed in the circle was a little overwhelming:

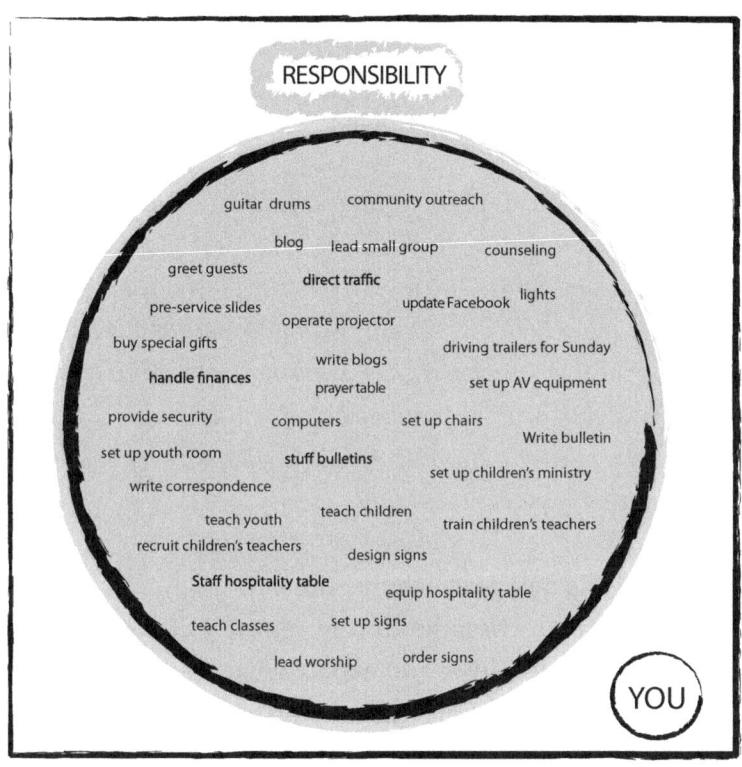

> "Their responsibility is to equip God's people to do his work and build up the church, the body of Christ."
> Ephesians 4:12 (NLT)

I told them I had a choice, as do all leaders, to do it myself and only accomplish a little of what needs to be done or to empower them as leaders to do ministries so that more gets accomplished. *Each leader has the same choice: grow a team and keep passion, excitement and energy in their lives or try to do it all themselves and burn out.*

> **THINK ABOUT IT.** *Each leader should have a co-leader and a team; no ministry should be just one person. It will be a seasonal ministry if it only has one person leading it. It takes more than one person to build a lasting ministry. Christ built a team because he knew he was on a timeline and he wanted to see ministry while he was here AND through eternity. The only way to do that was by having a team that would outlast him.*

We meet needs and make connections through ministry. We need to be able to breathe during ministry if we are going to invest in people's lives and expect what we do to last. We cannot do that if we are always running on empty, trying to do it alone.

RESPONSIBILITY TO RECRUIT

Every ministry has the responsibility to recruit. If the ministry role is greater than you or your team, you are in trouble and burnout is on the horizon. It's just a matter of time. If your ministry responsibilities are larger than you or your team, then the ministry itself will burn out, and the original passion will have its life sucked out by the responsibilities. We need to avoid that, so we need to keep track of where our level of passion is, and continue to build our teams to be larger than our responsibilities. If that happens, there will be ongoing excitement and strength, needs will be met and everyone will feel they are part of the journey. Our goal is to build a lasting ministry that will continue to accommodate people and avoid miserable feelings, frustrations or the negative thoughts that burnout creates. *Our goal is for ministry to last and to never burn out!*

We want to recruit volunteers in a relational way. That means that we meet people both before and after services, in small groups, in our discipleship classes, events and even throughout the community—and begin to develop relationships! You

*Building a **ministry** that will outlast you requires a **team** that will outlast you!*

know where this is headed. At our church, we needed to jump out of that box that kept the ministry leaders behind tables or hidden in their seats. We put them out on our patio before and after services, meeting people, getting to know who attends, who is plugged in as a volunteer, and who isn't, but even more importantly, who is visiting from the community and needs to connect with Christ! The fact that volunteers and ministry leaders are seeking new volunteers also puts them in front of the visiting community, making them feel like they are being welcomed into a church that cares. Do you see how it works? Leaders are developing relationships that grow and mature our church members *and* their teams.

PREPARING THE SOIL

It's important that you take the time to prepare the soil. The sower (leader) can do something about the seed but can't control the weather. The leader *can* control how he or she leads, and give their followers the best opportunity for success. So, I get to prepare the soil—to decide how well to prepare it. If it's not prepared, the weeds, the sun, and rocks will ruin the opportunity for growth.

> *"Then he taught them many things by using stories. He said, 'A farmer went out to scatter seed in a field. While the farmer was scattering the seed, some of it fell along the road and was eaten by birds. Other seeds fell on thin, rocky ground and quickly started growing because the soil wasn't very deep. But when the sun came up, the plants were scorched and dried up, because they did not have deep roots. Some other seeds fell where thornbushes grew up and choked the plants. But a few seeds did fall on good ground where the plants produced 100 or 60 or 30 times as much as was scattered. If you have ears, pay attention!... Now listen to the meaning of the story about the farmer: The seeds that fell along the road are the people who hear the message about the kingdom, but don't understand it. Then the evil one comes and snatches the message from their hearts. The seeds that fell on rocky ground are the people who gladly hear the message and accept it at once.*

> *But they don't have deep roots, and they don't last very long. As soon as life gets hard or the message gets them in trouble, they give up. The seeds that fell among the thorn-bushes are also people who hear the message. But they start worrying about the needs of this life and are fooled by the desire to get rich. So the message gets choked out, and they never produce anything. The seeds that fell on good ground are the people who hear and understand the message. They produce as much as 100 or 60 or 30 times what was planted."* Matthew 13:3-9; 18-23 (CEV)

The soil is a person. My preparation of each person, or lack of preparation for the role they will play, will determine how well they are doing. I don't put potential into people, but as a leader I need to draw the potential out of an individual.

I can give them a lot or a little responsibility, so I have to decide well. It can be a thirty minute per week role, or it can be a five-hour role. It's important that I prepare them appropriately for their roles and the opportunities I plan to give them to make decisions. People start with a zero time commitment and then grow into a small commitment, then a little more and more until at times, a massive number of hours may be spent.

How they expand into their role depends on how the soil is prepared—how you develop the relationship. The same person, if given too much all at once, might walk away, burned

To expand your organization and its potential, focus on growing leaders.

out. So I don't want to start them with too much responsibility. I want to see people grow into their ministry, rather than walk away from it because they are buried in an enormous amount of responsibility, without a process or preparation for doing their work. From then on, they would view ministry as a waste of time and would be unlikely to ever want to volunteer again. I want to err on the side of setting them up for success rather than failure.

My responsibility is to prepare the soil. God determines when to bring them to what commitment, but if they are brought to too great a commitment too soon, and they burn out, I may blame the person rather than myself as a leader. As a leader I have to be aware of the responsibility I delegate and the relationship I am nurturing.

People are often afraid to commit. They want to know who they are working with. They need to develop trust and believe in the leader. We don't want to overload or overwhelm them by making the mistake of passing on too much. People are afraid of being burned by being tasked with too much responsibility. In the church, this shouldn't be the case, but it happens.

"God has given each of you a gift from his great variety of spiritual gifts. Use them well to serve one another."
1 Peter 4:10 (NLT)

Once a connection is made and a relationship is built, then a *small responsibility should be given before a larger one.* There needs to be buy-in from them. Ask them, "How are you doing?" and listen to them. If they are doing okay, working within their comfort zone at an appropriate responsibility level, they may be ready for *more* responsibility. When they break out of their comfort zone, they may be afraid of the next step. You need to help them overcome that fear and give them a sense of security. "I know you can do it, I believe in you, you are gifted in this area..."

Leaders: work plus praise increases energy; work without praise drains energy. Energize those who work with you.

People by nature may talk themselves out of being used by God instead of INTO being used by God. It is your role as a leader to encourage, support, reinforce, love them and walk them through their fears.

RECRUITING RELATIONALLY
Here are some principles that work to assist a leader in recruiting volunteers and other leaders effectively in a relational way.

1. CAST VISION. A leader must cast the vision for what a volunteer does and how it influences the vision of the church and the lives of the people they are trying to impact.

For example, our traffic ministry isn't just about parking cars. It's about being the front door to someone who wants to try out change in his or her life. The volunteers are influencing those who are planning to come as well as those who were not planning to attend. They are the first impression of our church, and we only have one try at making that first impression. People will judge our church based on their first experience. The traffic ministry leader should have conversations when he or she is recruiting and understand well how the ministry fits into the church's vision. They are not just guys or girls in fluorescent vests standing out there, they are creating an important first impression of our church. They are the first people others see when they drive by, and decide to give us a try. There is where the relationship begins.

STORY: *We were looking for people to serve in our traffic ministry, but even though we were finding people to step in each week, there weren't any volunteers who were willing to "stick" with the ministry. I decided to talk with some of the volunteers one on one. Jerry told me, as we began our meeting, that he was hoping to "not" serve. He thought he wanted to do something different. I explained why the traffic ministry is important because of its impact on our campus as the first impression people have of our church. Prior to our meeting he had thought, "Am I doing anything?" I told him that the traffic ministry has an unspoken value in people's lives. That smiling and waving makes a difference and communicates joy and acceptance, relationships and hope that might be found if they visit. All that is communicated through a smile and a wave. Once Jerry understood the place of the traffic ministry in the vision of the church, he was glad to serve.*

Likewise, set up and tear down ministries have had an impact on the people who heard, experienced God's presence and accepted Christ or recommitted their lives to him that weekend. Setting up is all about unconnected people who would not have the opportunity to hear if there was no place to receive them.

In the same way, *every* ministry leader should be able to communicate how everything they do fits into the vision of the church, how and why it matters and why they are personally involved. If we don't know how a ministry fits into the vision of the church, then we shouldn't be doing it.

2. VALUE THE PERSON. Everyone's ability and desire to serve is different, at different times in their lives. Some can make a one hour weekly commitment, some six hours and some even twenty-five hours of service. A ministry leader needs to be aware of how volunteers can be used, regardless of the length of time they are able to serve. They need to know why they are important on the team, and what part they can play. They won't make a commitment if they don't feel as

though the hours they invest matter. Give an appropriately sized job for the time people have to spend.

Too many times I have seen leaders and team members become frustrated when the leader asks a team member to handle a responsibility that requires ten hours a week, but the team member only has TWO hours a week to complete that responsibility! The difference is an eight hour gap of frustration causing them to feel ignored, defiant, insecure and all the other thoughts a volunteer feels when a responsibility delegated didn't get accomplished. In reality, the leader should have never given a ten hour responsibility to someone who only has two hours to give. He should have had a relationship with them that was close enough to know how much time was available.

> *"All of you together are one body of Christ and each of you is a separate and necessary part of it."*
> 1 Corinthians 12:27
> (LB)

3. **COMPLIMENT THE INDIVIDUAL.** Build relationships with your team members and potential team members. Find out what's great about each of them as individuals and build them up, say positive things, recognize their talent and skills. Build a relationship and compliment them for the results you see. Learn to tell your team members about the good you see in them. People don't hear that enough in their lives. Time invested in people is never time wasted, even if you

aren't the one who sees the "return" on your time. Keep in mind that investing in people was God's idea!

We need to put "deposits" into each other's lives. It's like a "love bank," that helps us feel valued. We need to be aware that not everyone has the same banking values. In the case of my marriage, what makes me feel valued is not the same as what my wife needs to hear or experience to feel valued. We need to be sure we are making deposits appropriate for each other. My wife loves flowers, texts that encourage her, cuddle time, talking to her, and notes that intentionally express my love for her. Those all have high value in making her feel appreciated and loved. For me, please don't send me email or letters. No flowers. I value recreational things like tickets to a baseball game, coming to my sporting events, gathering my friends or her wanting to spend time with me—those things are deposits into my love bank and can help to build our marriage. The same goes for relationships with our leaders and teams. People are not the same, and we need to take the time to learn what feeds their individual love bank, and be intentional about making the investment in them.

> *"We should keep on encouraging each other to be thoughtful and to do helpful things."*
> Hebrews 12:24 (CEV)

> *What makes me feel valued is not the same as what my wife needs to hear or experience to feel valued.*

The reality is that we need to know volunteers well enough

> *"The Spirit's presence is shown in some way in each person for the good of all."*
> 1 Corinthians 12:7 (GNT)

to understand when and what we can ask of them, and what might cause them to burn out! Be careful that the "ask" isn't greater than the investment you have made in your leader's life. Never forget that we all work for the Kingdom of God and everyone deserves the investment.

4. PREPARE FOR OPPOSITION. One of the ways I have seen many leaders lose a potential team member is by not preparing them for opposition after personally asking them to join a serving team. Everyone will face a storm if they are

> *Your greatest life messages will come out of your hurts, not your strengths.*

committed; they are stepping out for the Kingdom of God. They should be told that they are doing something significant, and therefore will face opposition. There will be challenges.

When people feel a sense of ownership of a ministry, the church is THEIR church where relationships are being built and there *will be* opposition. Satan is fine with people sitting and soaking in church. When they start to participate is when he is not happy and that is when he sends opposition. God allows it to ultimately grow our character and faith.

Challenges team members are likely to face include those involving their time or relationships; or they may be presented with physical or financial challenges. A potential volunteer needs to be made aware of and prepared for the things that will arise and keep them from being used by God to be a bridge to others who don't know Christ. They should also know that as a leader, you will help them face the challenges.

5. ASK THEM FOR A COMMITMENT. Start with three months, six months or a year so that everyone knows the expectations. It will involve risk.

Remember when David was given the responsibility of simply watching sheep? With that simple responsibility, he had to learn how to fight off wolves, then he had to learn how to fight off bears, then lions. Once he conquered those responsibilities, he was then given the opportunity to fight off one of the most feared men who ever lived, Goliath! Once God took him through his slow, progressive leadership development, he then gave him the largest responsiblity he would ever face for his people: he was given the responsibility to be king of Israel. Imagine, it all started with being asked to take care of some sheep!

> *"...He raised up David to be their king, concerning whom He also testified and said, "I have found David the son of Jesse, a man after my own heart, who will do my will."*
>
> Acts 13:22 (NASB)

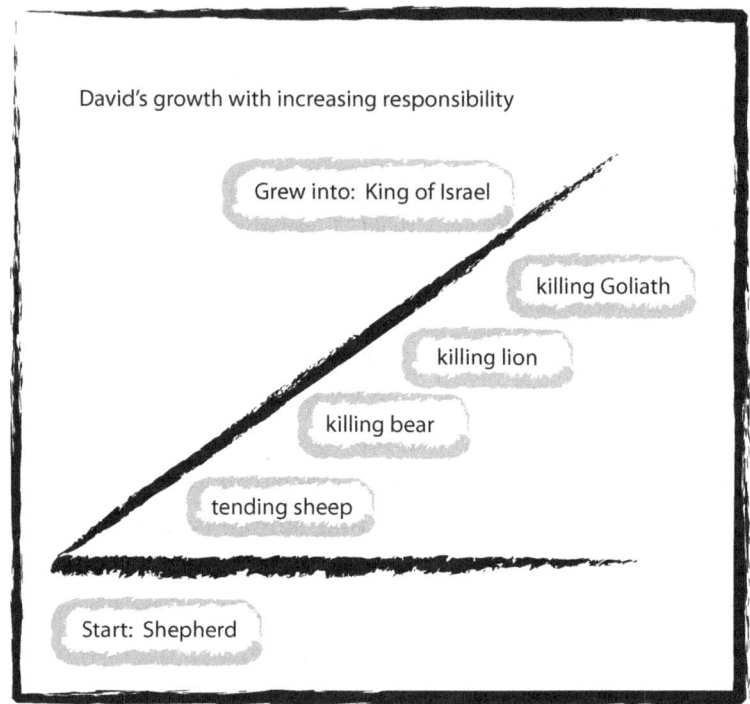

David's growth with increasing responsibility

Grew into: King of Israel

killing Goliath

killing lion

killing bear

tending sheep

Start: Shepherd

> *"The most important thing to remember is this: to be ready at any moment to give up what you are for what you might become.*   W.E.B. DuBois

Sometimes people are serving in the church, benefiting others, but when it comes to leadership they say, "I can't do that!" People need to be connected to the local church. It is relationships that bring people to church, to walk in and have a conversation, then trust God, take the opportunity to commit their lives to Him, then be baptized, and be encouraged in leadership and become part of the process. If they don't continue into leadership through relationships, they lose the opportunity to see life change in themselves and others. If God is in it, the lives of others will be changed, even if we are not in that role. It doesn't depend entirely on us, but God does allow us to experience the joy of seeing someone's life change by assuming leadership, and investing in relationships themselves.

> *Unless you try to do something beyond what you already mastered, you will never grow.*

Time-defined commitments allow for check-point conversations to have clarity, understanding and an opportunity for redirecting, refocusing and realignment if necessary.

Having check-point conversations allows you to talk openly about whether or not the volunteer is feeling valued, validated and most importantly, challenged. People need to be challenged in their involvement in ministry.

> *"If you are not willing to risk the unusual, you will have to settle for the ordinary."*
> *Jim Rohn*

Ministry is about making a difference, helping others move forward in their journey with Christ. It's not at all about passing time and going through the motions. Can you name any ministry that gets the *least* from the leaders/volunteers and is the best ministry? Can you name any organization, business or non-profit that gets the *least* from the people running it and are the best at what they do? Heck, can you name *anything* that gets the *least* from the people and are the best at what they do? No marriage will ever be great when the couple gives their *least*. No sports team has ever won a championship when the team gives their *least*. No teacher has ever received the best work from students who do their *least*.

> *Your character and integrity will be measured before your skill and experience. Who you are will always come before what you're capable of.*   Anonymous

MOVING VOLUNTEERS TO THEIR SWEET SPOTS
It was not threatening for the disciples to come to Christ. It was the next steps that put fear into them. You and I make a personal commitment to Christ, but we are afraid to take on more leadership responsibility because we are afraid we will let other people down. When we take up leadership, other people are relying on us and we are helping them to develop their God-given gifts. It's a different, more challenging spiritual journey as we help them find their "sweet spots" for ministry. It is a journey that deserves the best from whatever time allotment they have committed to, whether it's 15 hours, 5 hours, 10 hours or 40 hours, it is not the amount of time,

but the quality they are giving/getting from that time commitment. If the quality isn't present in a volunteer's specific ministry, transferring ministries should be a conversation that happens for their sake and the sake of the ministry.

Sometimes a volunteer isn't in the right position, and it's clear that they need to be somehow transitioned to something that suits their gifts and talents better, even if they enjoy what they are doing.

This is a difficult decision for a leader to make. There have been times when my desire to fill a leadership role has been greater than my desire to find the right leader for that position. I created problems for myself that could have been avoided if I would have been more *When desperation rises, standards fall.* patient and more intentional about finding the right fit. *When desperation rises, standards fall,* and I have definitely, at times, allowed my standards for the right leader to fall. The devil has the most influence when you are not in the calmest of moments—if you are not resting, at peace, thinking clearly. That is when you start thinking that it might be easier to not be married or to be done with this church family and *Choosing a team member is much easier than transferring one.* all the responsibility it requires. We allow these thoughts to give birth in our minds to the thought that life would simply be easier if we quit, weren't married, etc. When desperation rises, peace and joy falls, and God's place in my life is taken. I can save myself an awkward conversation, and might save people from feeling neglected, hurt and abandoned. When choosing a leader, choose *slowly, carefully,* in the context of a relationship. Choosing a team member is much easier than transferring one.

Redirect them to another place of ministry. Take the reigns back yourself. Shift them somewhere else on your team if possible, or to another ministry. Help cast the vision to them for what's next in their lives.

Pray. Don't venture into changing people's roles without prayer. Let God orchestrate the change by allowing team members time to do it before you take action. Be intentional about praying for the change, then be intentional about having enough conversations to allow the individual to share what is going on in their lives.

> **THINK ABOUT IT.** *If someone has a gift, we should provide an opportunity for them to serve. What are their passions? How can we create an opportunity so that their passion is fulfilled? No one was created without the ability to meet a need and serve in an area of passion. Serving allows for development of spiritual depth that will have a lasting mark on people's lives in a way that only "doing" can accomplish. You can learn what serving does*

to your life by reading about it or hearing about it—but this kind of spiritual growth only comes through doing it.

MISSING THE VISION

There is diversity in teams, but sometimes there are people who tend to distract from the direction of the church and its current capacity for ministry. That's a problem.

There is a problem with four things:

1. Understanding the vision of the church.

2. Understanding the direction, timing, and energy resources available for accomplishing the focus of the church.

3. The timing of what they are feeling God wants them to do.

For example, we had a volunteer who was passionate about starting a 12 step recovery program, but he was sensitive and willing to wait for the right timing. The right time + the right people + the right place = waiting on God's direction. It took two years for all the pieces to come together, but success was worth the wait.

This reminds me of the story of Joseph in Genesis chapters 37-47. He was a boy who was given a vision for what God was going to do in his life, but didn't get to see that vision come to fruition until he was in his late thirties—over twenty years later! The time God speaks to you about doing something in your life and when he actually brings it to pass may not always coincide. There may be a time gap. There is a fourth problem as well.

4. Does God want them to do something in a different church body?

Another volunteer believed he had a ministry that needed to start right away. He had put all the pieces together, but didn't understand the vision or direction of the church, and was in a rush to implement his own timetable, ignoring anything else that was happening at our campus. He was single mindedly convinced that he was filling an important gap. Ultimately his unwillingness to take into account the timing, or the overall vision for the church resulted in having to tell him that perhaps the timing wasn't right or that we weren't the right church body for his ministry.

There has to be a willingness to change for the sake of our relationship with Christ. If not, we will be stuck in part of the journey, but will not allow ourselves to be used for the whole journey. We can't miss the vision! It's the first step in our leadership growth.

Leaders will tend to look out for themselves unless you remind them who you ultimately are looking out for.

It's important to verbalize the vision's expectations, and it's important to allow the volunteers the freedom to agree or disagree. There is no need for a volunteer to demand that all of their expectations be met. Building the team is important to team health, and discussion is healthy. It's part of the relationship

Earlier in my career our church relocated one of our ministries to a new spot on campus. The ministry leader was clearly upset, and came to me and asked if we could put it back where it "belonged." It was too difficult for people to see, he thought, but back in its original location, "it was just better for the volunteers." Then came the subtle threat, "I don't know how much longer I can do this." The mistake was that he hadn't been brought on board to understand the philosophy of the relocation. Our vision to reach the unreached had everything to do with the move. Ultimately, it had been a decision that supported the vision to serve the unchurched rather than the desires of the long-time churched.

There may be a time when someone isn't connecting with the vision and is making everyone else crazy with the discord that they ferment. They need to be given biblically appropriate warnings and then as a leader, you should ask them to step down from their position if they continue to cause disunity. Scripture tells us to live in unity.

"As a prisoner of the Lord, I beg you to live in a way that is worthy of the people God has chosen to be his own. Always be humble and gentle. Patiently put up with each other and love each other. Try your best to let God's Spirit keep your hearts united. Do this by living at peace. All of you are part of the same body. There is only one Spirit of God, just as you were given one hope when you

> *were chosen to be God's people. We have only one Lord, one faith, and one baptism. There is one God who is the Father of all people. Not only is God above all others, but he works by using all of us, and he lives in all of us."*
> Ephesians 4:1-6

When conflict arises and someone expresses their belief that God is speaking to them directly as to the direction the church needs to be going, remind them that we as volunteers and leaders are responsible to support the vision God has placed on the lead pastor. Heresy not included, God is serious about unity and it's unlikely he would skip the pastor and instead give a vision, focus or direction to a church member to communicate to the leaders or senior pastor of the church. Seldom is a member used to get the pastor on track with God's vision. Instead, when this is attempted, it creates discord.

Unfortunately, this has happened to me. Once a member from the church felt strongly about starting a ministry that wasn't a part of our vision. Another time a ministry wasn't being accomplished the way the volunteer thought it should.

In both cases those individuals needed to have an informative vision conversation with me. If their idea for ministry had fallen in line with the direction of the church, and their plans were sound, then what simply needed to happen was to pray for the right leader and for the timing of the ministry.

Once all of that becomes clear, then you can allow them to test or practice the ministry before going public. That means that everything falls in line: the timing, direction, and focus. I have seen churches and leaders go "public" in the church and the community too soon, and then find out that the timing wasn't right or the leader wasn't right for the ministry. Sometimes both. That puts you in the awkward position of explaining to people why the ministry needs to be put on hold or will no longer exist. It can be avoided if the first three steps take place: direction (vision), focus and timing.

Sometimes there is a member who has a passion to start a ministry that doesn't fall in line with the vision of the church, or it falls in line, but the timing isn't right. It sounds easier than it is, but here is the amazing answer: ask them to put the ministry on hold, and wait for the right timing.

It's not often that upcoming leaders can appreciate the word, "wait", "hold on," "not yet," "soon, but not now" or any other combination of words to indicate a yellow or red light.

I have had leaders create conflict and disunity after being told they had to wait for the right timing. When they begin to poison the church by communicating that leadership is not supporting their dreams and visions, we have a big problem.

> *When a fool is annoyed, he quickly lets it be known.*
> *Wise people will ignore an insult.*
> Proverbs 12:16 (GNT)

Nehemiah had these same issues thousands of years ago when rebuilding the wall and the leaders were taking advantage of the poor. Scenarios change but the same problems of human nature continue to arise. We will always struggle with not having our way. It starts when we are children. My two and three year olds struggle with waiting. A common phrase when they have to wait for a toy, ice cream or to play is, "No, I want it now!" We grow up but those things don't change much.

In chapter 5 of Nehemiah, he handled disunity well:

> "⁶When I heard their complaints and their charges, I became very angry. ⁷So I thought it over and said to the leaders and officials, 'How can you charge your own people interest?' Then I called a public meeting and accused the leaders ⁸by saying, 'We have tried to buy back all of our people who were sold into exile. But here you are, selling more of them for us to buy back!' The officials and leaders did not say a word, because they knew this was true. ⁹I continued, 'What you have done is wrong! We must honor our God by the way we live, so the Gentiles can't find fault with us. ¹⁰My relatives, my friends, and I are also lending money and grain, but we must no longer demand payment in return. ¹¹Now give back the fields, vineyards, olive orchards and houses you have taken and also the interest you have been paid.'

> ¹²*The leaders answered, 'We will do whatever you say and return their property, without asking to be repaid.' So I made the leaders promise in front of the priests to give back the property.* ¹³*Then I emptied my pockets and said, 'If you don't keep your promise, that's what God will do to you, He will empty out everything you own, even taking away your houses.' The people answered, 'We will keep our promise.' Then they praised the Lord and did as they had promised."* Nehemiah 5:6-13 (CEV)

1. Nehemiah took it seriously. In verse 6 he didn't ignore the problem, or look the other way. He took disunity very seriously.

2. He used words carefully. In verse 7, Nehemiah didn't allow his first emotions to be his first words. He became angry but then "thought it over" and allowed himself to ponder the problem.

3. He met one on one first in verse 7. There was no maneuvering or spiritualizing the situation. He went straight to those who were causing disunity and confronted them.

4. He led by example in verse 12, Nehemiah modeled what he expected to see from the people. When he asked them to rebuild the wall, it was because *he* was already rebuilding it. When he asked them to no longer demand payment, verse 10 tells us *he* had already stopped demanding payment. Nehe-

miah never asked anyone to do what he wasn't already doing or willing to do. Neither should leaders.

> *"...warn a divisive person once, and then warn him a second time. After that, have nothing to do with them. You may be sure that such people are warped and sinful; they are self-condemned."*   Titus 3:10-11 (NIV)

5. He warned, then recommited and they praised the Lord together in verse13.

> **THINK ABOUT IT.** *"As God delays, you'll face two types of difficulties: circumstances and critics. This is a natural part of life. God designed it this way...we grow stronger when facing adversity and opposition.*
>
> *When Moses led the children of Israel out of Egypt into the desert toward the Promised Land, he had one problem after another. First there was no water. Then there was no food. Then there were a bunch of complainers. Then there were poisonous snakes. Moses was doing what God wanted him to do, but he still had problems.*
>
> *Having a dream doesn't mean not facing challenges; challenges are part of any growing process. There is no growth without being stretched."*   Unknown

Unfortunately, this ugly side of ministry—having to warn those who cause discontent—is not the reason anyone says yes to ministry, but is very much a reality of maintaining unity.

One of my least favorite things to do with my children is discipline them. I would love it if they would just always do the right thing, keep themselves and others safe and I could just play with them and have all the fun children bring to the family. Unfortunately, they are human, and need direction in what is right, wrong, safe and unsafe. In order for parents to enjoy those moments that melt your heart, we need to also have those moments that keep children aligned with what is right and safe. The same is true of ministry and the volunteers you will lead.

Moses struggled with discontent when the people of Israel got tired of waiting when he went up to the mountain to talk with God.

"After the people saw that Moses had been on the mountain for a long time, they went to Aaron and said, "Make us an image of a god who will lead and protect us. Moses brought us out of Egypt, but nobody knows what has happened to him." Aaron told them, "Bring me the gold earrings that your wives and sons and daughters are wearing." Everybody took off their earrings and brought them to Aaron, then he melted them and made an idol

> *in the shape of a young bull. All the people said to one another, "This is the god who brought us out of Egypt.*
> Exodus 32:1-4 (CEV)

When he took too long, in their estimation, they felt strongly they needed to move forward and choose a new god. They talked about their frustration with each other, communicated their discontent with enough people, and they collectively arrived at what seemed to be a good idea. They built a new god of gold!

It's interesting how we read about this and think, "That is so stupid. How can you abandon the direction of God and the leadership of Moses and replace God with a gold statue?" Yet, it happens every day and it happens in every church.

We will always have disagreements in the church. It's okay and expected not to agree on everything, but what is **not** okay is disunity. God expects unity in the midst of disagreements in the church.

WHEN TO SAY "NO" TO STAY FOCUSED ON THE VISION

Recruiting should always support the vision. When ministries are forming and leaders are looking for team members, it is important to maintain their focus on accomplishing the vision. They may need to say, "no" to things that have the potential to derail them from that focus.

> *"When evening came, after the sun had set, they began bringing to Him all who were ill and those who were demon-possessed. And the whole city had gathered at the door. And He healed many who were ill with various diseases, and cast out many demons; and He was not permitting the demons to speak, because they knew who He was.*
>
> *In the early morning, while it was still dark, Jesus got up, left the house, and went away to a secluded place, and was praying there. Simon and his companions searched for Him; they found Him and said to Him, "Everyone is looking for You." He said to them, **"Let us go somewhere else to the towns nearby, so that I may preach there also; for that is what I came for."***
>
> Mark 1:32-38 (NASB)

As a leader, people want you to meet their needs, but you need to stay true to the vision, even if that means you will not meet all of their expectations. Jesus was doing what he loved best: loving the people, healing the sick, mending the broken, and giving hope to the hopeless. Obviously the word had gotten out and when the people heard that the Christ was in town, they surrounded the house where he had been because they too had needs they wanted him to meet. Yet, what did Jesus say

> *"Never doubt in the dark what God told you in the light."*
> Raymond Edman

to the disciples when they told him that there was a mass of people who wanted to spend time with him? He said to them, *"Let us go somewhere else...".*

Jesus focused on Jerusalem when the time for his sacrifice was drawing near—he needed to stay true to the journey. As he was headed in that direction, teaching and preaching along the way, he also had to say no to healing people who were in need. If he had lingered along the road to heal everyone who wanted a touch from him, he would not have been in Jerusalem for the Passover and for his ultimate sacrifice for the world. He said no to the village, one mission field, for the sake of the greater mission: the world. Beginning with Luke 9:51, he was resolutely on his way to Jerusalem.

> *"As the time approached for Him to be taken up to heaven, Jesus resolutely set out for Jerusalem."* Luke 9:51 (NIV)

It's hard to say no to all the good ministries, events and activities there are to engage us, but as leaders, it is crucial that we stay focused on the vision, and therefore crucial that the vision for the whole church be passed down to the ministry leaders and every volunteer. If that happens, the church will "feel" it, everyone will be able to breathe, and duplication will be ongoing as the members grow in spiritual maturity.

Jesus knew his boundaries: when to say yes and when to say no. People were always in his face, always surrounding him. I tend to be able to say no when I know what I have said yes to. If I don't know what I have said yes to, then I don't know how to say no and can quickly become overwhelmed with too much.

People always NEED you as a leader and want more time with you. You hear things like, "I need...," "Are you going to?" "I want..." "I *must* meet with you." "Can you...?" "Will you...?" "I feel you should..." These are words leaders will always hear. That's how it was with Christ.

> "One man can be a crucial ingredient on a team, but no man can make a team."
>
> Kareem Abdul Jabbar.

Christ had said yes to the destination, he knew where he was going. He had a goal, and that was Jerusalem and the cross. But through the journey there was ministry. His focus was to build the church and to build people. In that process, he was constantly moving toward the goal.

The more a leader has to do, the more important it is to say yes to God's vision for your ministry, and no to the things other people can handle. In the process of getting there you will build the church and build people. When you say yes to God's vision, you are more likely to say no to the demands and distractions and even "good things" that come up on a daily basis. We need to be directly focused on how to help people along the way as we seek to fulfill God's vision.

At a leadership meeting, Rick Warren shared a story about pruning a fruit tree in his yard that was producing a lot of little fruit. He had to prune away that little fruit so that bigger fruit could grow. The result was fewer fruit, but those which grew were bigger. And so with ministry, sometimes we need to prune away the little things we are doing to see the bigger things that God is doing come to fruition. That is why team-building is so important.

> **THINK ABOUT IT:** *One of the dangers of enjoying a particular aspect of your ministry is that it takes you away from what only YOU can do as a leader. Ultimately you need to allow others to do the things that others can do. Know your leaders well enough to know when you can delegate to them. Why not ask someone who is good at what you need to have done, and allow them to do it instead of doing it yourself? You will ultimately use your day better. Remember, only YOU can be the leader. Sometimes we're afraid of being rejected, so we just don't ask. The consequence is that we sacrifice the growth of our ministry for the maintenance of the church. Both need to happen, and both CAN through leaders who have made an investment in those they lead.*

STORY: *A pastor friend of mine called one day, exasperated that he had spent five hours searching for a round table and chairs for his platform at church. I asked him why he hadn't asked a leader or volunteer to do it. He said, "I never thought about that! Do you think I should do that?" Of course he could ask a leader or volunteer to search out a table and chairs for him! He had taken five hours out of his day doing what a volunteer could have done better, and probably a lot faster. That was time lost and you will always be short on time when you don't allow the team to do things they can do better and faster than you.*

If you are stressed by your to-do list, you are doing things you weren't meant to do; you only have time to do the things you were meant to do.

R.E.D.
EQUIPPING

TIME

It's all about time. Leaders need to spend time together with their teams. If people feel as though the leader gives direction, guidance and cares for the team members, they are more likely to feel ownership in their positions.

> *"He comforts us in all our troubles so that we can comfort others. When they are troubled, we will be able to give them the same comfort God has given us."*
> 1 Corinthians 2:4 (NLT)

We need to spend most of our time equipping leaders. Our goal is to build leaders to look more like Christ. Jesus built a team. He personally recruited his team, built relationships and painted a picture of how he would accomplish his goals. He spent three years with them, 24/7—he was constantly with them. He allowed them to watch him. They did ministry together, and then he watched them minister on their own. He taught them in crowds, he taught them in small groups, and he taught them one on one. The concept was basically like this: "I do it" — "we do it together" — "you do it while I watch." It was a model worth repeating.

Jesus had three key leaders: Peter, James and John.

> *"And there came a man named Jairus, and he was an official of the synagogue; and he fell at Jesus' feet, and began to implore Him to come to his house; for he had an only daughter, about twelve years old, and she was dying...While He was still speaking, someone came from the house of the synagogue official, saying, 'Your daughter has died; do not trouble the Teacher anymore.' But when Jesus heard this, He answered him, 'Do not be afraid any longer; only believe, and she will be made well.' When He came to the house, He did not allow anyone to enter with him, except **Peter and John and James**, and the girl's father and mother. Now they were all weeping and lamenting for her; but He said, 'Stop weeping, for she has not died, but is asleep.' And they began laughing at Him, knowing that she had died. He, however, took her by the hand and called, saying, 'Child, arise!' And her spirit returned, and she got up immediately; and He gave orders for something to be given her to eat. Her parents*

> *were amazed; but He instructed them to tell no one what*
> *had happened."* Luke 8:41-42; 49-56 (NASB)

I was struck that when the child died, *only these three were allowed into the room along with Jesus and her parents to see the miracle that was about to take place.* They were the only witnesses. The others were outside talking, I suppose, about things that had already been done: the miracles of the past, the "good ol' days," the highlights of their journey. But the three, those fortunate three, experienced the miracle personally with Jesus. While the others were outside talking about yesterday, the privileged three were in the room experiencing the power of God that day. They had greater understanding of the miracle as it was unveiled intimately rather than with a group of 12 or a crowd of 5,000. The difference was between being listeners or being participants. When Jesus taught the twelve, they were listeners, but when he taught them one on one, he allowed them to be participants, and more about the miracle was revealed to them.

From a leadership perspective, the power of one on one conversation is that those conversations give more opportunities to those who hear and see. If you are always speaking to a large crowd, then those in the crowd are only receivers of what's being said, rather than being accountable and sharing struggles. When a leader spends time with those he is leading, it allows them to watch him, to do things together, and then to have the confidence to do it themselves while you watch and cheer them on.

> *"Now that I, your Lord and Teacher, have washed your feet, you also should wash one another's feet. I have set you an example that you should do as I have done for you."* John 13:14-15 (NIV)

MEETING IN SMALL LEADERSHIP GROUPS

As a leader it is important to communicate the overall vision to those you lead. They want to know "Where are you taking us?" "What is my role in the big picture?" "How does what I do fit into the vision?" They need to have their questions answered. Small groups, in whatever form they take in your church, are the artery through which members grow into spiritual health. In small groups, a member's words, thoughts and actions indicate spiritual growth—or not. Are they connecting? Are people's commitments outlasting their emotions? Are they serving? Are they engaging in evangelism? What are they doing to reach those who don't know Christ? Are they holding each other accountable?

LEADING LEADERS INTO TEAM BUILDING.

I build a little more into our leaders each time we meet, reviewing what they have already been taught, affirming what they are doing right, and then giving them another bite.

Ministry leaders need to know the next steps for bringing people into their teams, but those steps shouldn't be communicated until they have relevance, and the need is felt. They should first have a picture of what they need, and then the freedom to do it on their own.

Jesus took the disciples out in the boat, knowing that they would face a storm. The boat was tossed in the waves, swamped, but it was then in the midst of their fear and faithlessness that Jesus taught them about faith. It's important to know what to give your leaders during the four phases of their lives:

1. Sitting on the shore enjoying the view of the sun reflecting on the water.
2. Going on a boat ride out into the middle of the water, enjoying the wind in your face and the smooth rocking of the boat.
3. During the storm of their lives when it just doesn't feel like it's ever going to end and there is no way out.
4. Coming out of the big black hole of a storm with a sigh of relief, clear air, feeling of gratitude for life!

You are always balancing when to teach while they are in each of those four conditions. I don't always get it right.

THINK ABOUT IT: *It's always difficult to submit to God's timing. As a leader, you see before other see, and you see further than others see. Waiting is very hard, a constant battle.*

Remember, there is a particular timing for all things. Like the ocean, big and small waves come, but all follow a system.

It is the same with fruit trees. There is a time for growing roots and leaves and stems and there is a time for fruit-bearing. Of course, you are always waiting for the big set of waves, or the fruit to become a huge harvest. Sometimes, though, it's all about planting and watering and waiting for the growth. With waves, there is always the wait between sets; you don't see a big wave in every set.

COMMITTED AND FLEXIBLE

"Trust in the Lord with all your heart and do not lean on your own understanding. In all your ways acknowledge Him, and He will make your paths straight."

Proverbs 3:5-7(NASB)

Trust in the Lord. These verses remind me of God's system, and how He works in the lives of others. I need to give up my anxiety to the Lord, rely on His expectations, not mine. Then my self-inflicted expectations will go away. Of course, it's human nature to go back and be anxious again.

> STORY: *I had a relational task that I needed to ask one of my staff members to do. Lucy was the one that God had put on my heart to do the job, but because of her existing commitments, I was a little concerned that she wouldn't be willing to take it on. I was right. Lucy realized that accepting the responsibility would involve considerable time meeting with team members. "I really don't think I have time," she said. There were a LOT of reasons to say no, but Lucy agreed to pray about it. She came back the next week. "I'll try it for three months," she told me. When the provisional time was about over, I asked her how it was going. "GREAT!" she said with a smile. "I have been meeting with the leaders, and every time I do, it just energizes me! I LOVE it!"*

Even though Lucy was afraid of more responsibility, she found that when she was willing to be stretched into that position, God gave her more energy and passion for the task than she ever imagined possible.

> THINK ABOUT IT: *The baby, Ezra had the flu. He threw up at 9,11,1 and 6 and was SCARED! When he first threw up, Jill walked out of the bedroom with him,*

> covered in puke and handed him to me. I didn't even pay attention to the mess as Ezra grabbed hold of me and held on tight, his eyes wide. He had no idea what was happening to him. He was scared and just wanted to be close.
>
> In fearful moments we tend to grab on to what we believe to be the most secure. You are thinking and feeling, "I don't understand what is happening to me."

When we face fearful moments and experiences, we hold on to God because He is the most secure and safe. He understands the how and why of what has happened. He knows what the results will be and has any answer that we seek. We may not have the answers, but we do have a relationship with our Father. He is not surprised. I don't know what will happen, but God does.

> "Oh yes, you shaped me first inside, then out; you formed me in my mother's womb. I thank you, High God—you're breathtaking! Body and soul, I am marvelously made! I worship in adoration—what a creation! You know me inside and out, you know every bone in my body..."
> Psalm 139:13-15 (MSG)

God is in Control. It's exciting *because* God is in control. He is alive and the Holy Spirit is alive and miracles are still happening, even now. What we view as a problem, God views as an opportunity. I have an ongoing motto: **be committed to the goal, but be flexible in the process.** God changes processes.

> *Anybody can turn good into good, but only God can turn bad into good. Only He can turn a crucifixion into a resurrection.*

AFFIRMATION

As leaders, we sometimes get stuck in a certain process, thinking, "it has to be this way." When we do this to ourselves we often deviate from God's ultimate goal. God changes our view of how things are going to get done as reminders that His goal is not always *Be committed to the goal, but flexible in the process!* the same as our personal goals and his process may change..

When you affirm people, you raise their value. When you appreciate people, you raise their value. If you do it well, you can move them toward God's ultimate goals for your ministry. You can affirm people by listening. *Listen to them.*

> *"Share each others troubles and problems, and in this way obey the law of Christ."* Galatians 6:2 (NLT)

One of the greatest gifts you can give a person is an attentive ear. When you look someone straight in the eye and listen to him or her, it communicates, "I value you. I value what you have to say." *Use positive words.* They are much more likely to appreciate the process toward the goal.

> *"Do not use harmful words, but only helpful words, the kind that build up and provide what is needed, so that what you say will do good to those who hear you."*
> Ephesians 4:29 (TEV)

TEN THINGS TO ENCOURAGE AND AFFIRM YOUR TEAM:
1. Stay focused and have a clear vision.
2. Spend individual time with them.
3. Be open-minded. Encourage creativity, acknowledge the quality of the contribution.
4. Avoid poor planning and unproductive meetings.
5. Positive attitudes – be consistent and positive.
6. Show ongoing appreciation. People still want to be encouraged, even when they have accepted a responsibility and are settled in. If not, they will move on. What is rewarded is repeated.
7. Maximize people's potential. Develop a volunteer's potential, and encourage them to go from the ordinary to

the extraordinary. Spot a 10 who is functioning at a 2 and grow them to a 10 by investing in their lives.

8. Don't waste their time – help them to have a greater than average experience.

9. Focus on the true meaning of what we are doing. Remember why we are doing this.

10. Build connections – give them a sense of unity and involvement with the experience.

R.E.D.
DUPLICATING

D is for duplication. That is what we need to do: duplicate. Jesus called his disciples individually to be a part of his team, to be disciples.

> *As Jesus was walking beside the Sea of Galilee, he saw two brothers, Simon called Peter and his brother Andrew. They were casting a net into the lake, for they were fishermen. "Come, follow me," Jesus said, "and I will send you out to fish for people." At once they left their nets and followed him.*
>
> *Going on from there, he saw two other brothers, James son of Zebedee and his brother John. They were in a boat with their father Zebedee, preparing their nets. Jesus called them, and immediately they left the boat and their father and followed him.* Matthew 4:18 (NASB)

Jesus personally asked his disciples to be a part of the team—
and they said YES, dropping everything and walking with him
for three years. They watched Jesus do ministry, they did it
together with him, and then they did it on their own.

> STORY: *At our church Kathy's husband was a part of
> the set up team, arriving early every week to get ready
> for services. Week after week she attended, arriving later,
> just before the service started. She was uninvolved until
> one day one of the leaders mentioned to her that there was
> a need for more volunteers to stuff bulletins. She said,
> "I think I could do that." And so she arrived early, eager
> to learn how it was done. After that, the same leader
> mentioned that she needed someone to fill in for her oc-
> casionally to write the bulletin. Kathy had been watching,
> interested in where the inserts had come from. She said,
> "I think I could do that." The leader had been attentive,
> and soon Kathy and the leader sat side by side as the leader
> showed her how they were produced. The next week, Kathy
> tried it with the leader watching. They enjoyed lunch
> afterwards, and soon Kathy was able to do it on her own!*

The ministry leader had asked for help (R-Recruited). She
trained the volunteer how to help (E-Equipped), and then she
watched Kathy do it on her own (D-Duplicated). Before she
knew it she had built a team, simply because she had followed

the three simple steps to team building. The ministry went from "work" to enjoyment, all throughout the process.

> STORY: *The set up team had been struggling for awhile with just a few committed men. They were getting close to burnout and it was becoming drudgery instead of ministry to them. Josh decided that they needed to do something about the problem, so he started asking men one-on-one whether they might be able to be involved just one Sunday a month. About a dozen men said they would do it. However, they all said, "you will have to teach me." Each Sunday as they came to help, Josh showed them what to do. After a few times they were able to do it themselves, and soon they didn't want to miss out on the fun of working together to get things set up. Josh was simply duplicating himself, investing in the other men to lessen the burden of ministry alone.*

Josh had asked for help (R-Recruited), trained them how to help (E-Equipped), and then watched them do it on their own (D-Duplicated). Soon, he had built a team because he had started with these three simple steps to team building. His ministry went from exhaustion to excitement, throughout the team building process.

> *Building a team helps you move from breathless exhaustion to excitement.*

PREPARING DISCIPLES

Jesus knew he had a timeline for his ministry. He had a purpose, direction and a plan for how it would happen. His recruitment was personal, and he had a system for duplicating himself.

> "Come, follow me," Jesus said, "and I will send you out to fish for people." At once they left their nets and followed him.
> Matthew 4:18 (NASB)

I thought it odd that the disciples were one day engaged in doing the family business and then, "at once they left their nets and they followed him." I asked, "Why would they do that?" There was more to being a Jewish rabbi and saying, "Come, follow me" than what we see in this verse.

Being a Jewish rabbi was the most honored, respected position for a man in that culture. The goal of every Jewish boy was to be a rabbi. However, only 5% of the boys who aspired to that goal actually reached it. That means that 95% failed to become rabbis. The career path, then, for every boy was to TRY. There were three "schools" that the boys would go through:

*1. **Bet Safer**. Ages 6-10. Boys would memorize the Pentateuch, the first five books of the Torah. At some point the rabbis would pass around a plank of wood with honey on it for the students to taste, and then would tell them, "May the Word of God be like honey on your lips."*

The rabbis would evaluate each student, and at the end of the class select a special few, the cream of the crop, to go on to the second phase. Those selected were the best of the best, the special children who showed unique signs of giftedness. They would be told, "You have what it takes..." and though the others would be commended for their effort, they were told, "Go home to learn your family trade."

*2. **Bet Talmud.** Ages 10-15. Called the House of Learning, the students memorized the rest of the Old Testament. They were told, "This is your life!" The Scriptures consumed all of their lives. The rabbis were watching them, looking for the best. They observed how they thought, articulated words and expressed themselves. At the end of the school, the rabbis had made their decision, and those selected were allowed to move ahead to the third school. The remainder were told, "It is evident you love God and do a good job memorizing Scripture, knowing Scripture, even a decent job interpreting Scripture, but unfortunately you don't have what it takes to be a rabbi. You need to go home to learn your family trade."*

*3. **Bet Midrash.** 15-30 years old. The school was called the House of Study. In this school, the students chose a rabbi to follow. They examined the rabbis, listened to* *their philosophies, talked with them, for each one had his own "yoke." They were considering during their search, "Which rabbi would I want to be like; which one is the best 'fit' for me? Which rabbi could I duplicate?" When he had decided, the student would ask the rabbi if he could be his disciple. The rabbi would question the student about his life, his own philosophy, about what he knew from the Scriptures. He was looking to see if the young man had what it took to be his disciple. He was wondering, "Could he be ME?" If he thought the disciple could duplicate him, then he would tell the student, "Yes." If not, the student was told, "I'm sorry. I know you have done well with Scripture, you have done well with your studies, philosophy, interpretation, but unfortunately you don't have what it takes to be a rabbi." These students, too, were told to go home and learn the family trade.*

So, it was an enormous honor to be a disciple. Of COURSE when Jesus asked Peter and Andrew, they said yes! It was their second chance. They had been engaged in the family trade: fishing. They had missed the mark before, but now a prominent rabbi, Jesus, was asking them to be his disciple. Their father was okay with that, for it would make him very proud to have a son who had been asked to be a rabbi's disciple.

God has gifted each and every individual uniquely. What did Jesus see in the disciples that was uniquely attributed to them?

He looked for people who would say "yes" to Him. In the case of Jesus' disciples, He asked, and they said, "Yes."

Everyone has dreamed about having a second chance. Athletes wish for come-backs all the time. People go to school later in life and change careers; sometimes they have two or three in their lifetime rather than just one as was the norm years ago. All of this is because there is a desire for a second chance, to do something better or in a different way than before.

What the disciples saw when Jesus asked was a second chance. Each one had been rejected at some time during their training to be a rabbi and had been told to go back home and learn their family trade. Jesus was giving each one a second chance.

It lends a different perspective to think about discipleship and duplication in this way. When Jesus was gone, the needs were still being met, modeled, taught and watched. Here we are more than 2,000 years later, using the same process!

"Immediately he made His disciples get into the boat and go ahead of Him to the other side, while He sent the crowds away. He went up on the mountain by Himself to pray; and when it was evening He was there alone.

> *But the boat was already a long distance from the land, battered by the waves; for the wind was contrary. And in the fourth watch of the night He came to them, walking on the sea. When the disciples saw Him walking on the sea, they were terrified, and said, 'It is a ghost!' And they cried out in fear. But immediately Jesus spoke to them, saying, 'Take courage, it is I; do not be afraid.' Peter said to Him, 'Lord, if it is You, command me to come to You on the water. And He said, 'Come!' And Peter got out of the boat, and walked on the water and came toward Jesus."*
>
> Matthew 14:22-29 (NASB)

Why did Peter get out of the boat and do that? Why would he think that he could walk on the water? Peter was asked to be a disciple, so he trusted that the rabbi who had asked him believed that Peter could also walk on water. He thought, "If my rabbi can do it, then I should be able to do it as well." He was, in effect, being told by Jesus, "You can be me," and so of course if Jesus could, so could Peter. Peter believed he could, and so he did it—for a little while. When he relied on God, he DID walk on water!

What Jesus was ultimately doing was recruiting his team, equipping his leaders, and duplicating himself so he wouldn't be the only one doing ministry. He wouldn't be the only one relying on the power of God to do the impossible.

DUPLICATING

"R" is the process of gathering a team. You know you have reached this goal when you have people on your team who weren't there before you recruited them.

"E" is the process of equipping your team. You know you have reached this goal when you see your team doing things you used to do.

"D" is the process of duplicating yourself to do the ministry when you are not present. Once you arrive at this point, you know you have built a ministry that will outlast you!

This next story sounds very similar to what happened with Jarius' daughter. Long after Jesus' resurrection, Peter duplicated what he had seen Jesus do when he healed the synagogue official's daughter in Luke 8:41.

"Now in Joppa, there was a disciple named Tabitha...this woman was abounding with deeds of kindness and charity which she continually did. And it happened at that time that she fell sick and died; and when they had washed her body, they laid it in an upper room. Since Lydda was near Joppa, the disciples, having heard that Peter was there, sent two men to him, imploring him, 'Do not delay in coming to us.' So Peter arose and went with them. When he arrived, they brought him into the upper room; and all the widows stood beside him, weeping...But Peter sent them all out and knelt down and prayed, and turning to

> *the body, he said, 'Tabitha, arise.' And she opened her eyes and when she saw Peter, she sat up. And he gave her his hand and raised her up; and calling the saints and widows, he presented her alive.* Acts 9:36-41 (NASB)

This is what Jesus did. The process of having the disciples watch what he did, then do things together with him, and then on their own with Jesus' watching—that was all God's idea! When Peter was faced with a similar situation, he remembered what he had seen Jesus do, and in faith, did the same thing.

This is what duplicating yourself is: passing on your skills, heart, passion, everything about being you so that the work you have begun can continue whether or not you are involved. In this way, when your time is over in whatever ministry you are involved in, it will continue. Jesus equipped his disciples 24/7 for three years, so that when he was separated from the team he was preparing, they were ready! They were able to take all they had learned and duplicated his ministry of healing, teaching, addressing needs and calling people to come and serve.

> **THINK ABOUT IT:** *There is a difference between a "worker" and a "leader" mentality. A leader says, "Who can I train to do this?" A leader is unafraid to ask the question, "Will you...?"*

INVESTING IN LEADERS

As leadership clarity and commitment grows, it seems as though we should have fewer leadership problems. When a crisis arises, it is natural that I would ask, "What should I have done that could have avoided this?" "Did I not spend enough time with them? Did I not encourage them enough? Did I not meet with them one on one enough?"

Most of the time, conflicts arise when not enough time has been spent with leadership. Those you are trying to lead become more difficult to convince of change or renewed vision. There is less conflict that arises when you meet one on one more often. It's like planting a seed. You prepare the soil, plant the seed, water it, remove the weeds and nurture the small seedling until it matures into a full grown tree. Preparing the soil and nurturing the new plant was worth your time because the end resulted in a fruitful, mature tree. In the same way, your investment in people brings a return on your investment, for their value in ministry and leadership is far greater. If you spend little time, you will have grown low on stable leadership when problems arise. There is great value in investing one on one with key leaders. There was a reason that Christ spent time with the crowds, as well as one on one time with people. There was a return that resulted in groups of committed, focused disciples.

When obstacles arise, you change your direction to reach your goal; you do not change your decision to get there.

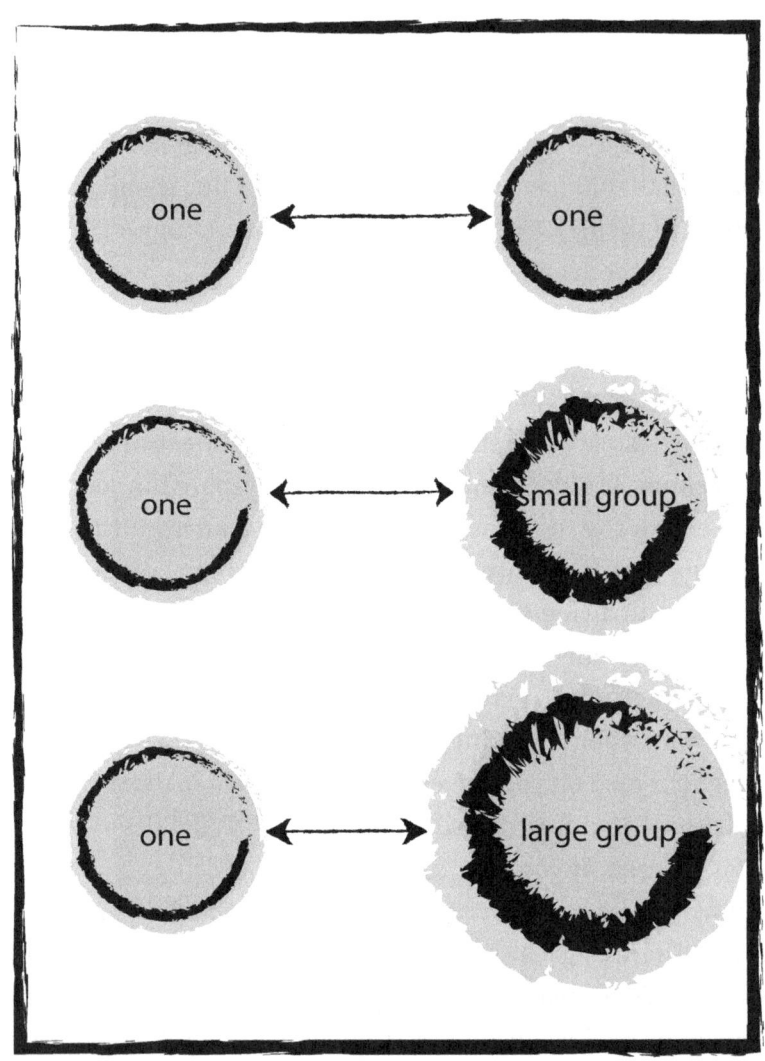

CLARITY IN LEADERSHIP

If no one is spending one on one time, there is little clarity. Sometimes leaders don't even know who they report to, have little commitment or understanding of the vision and lack leadership involvement in their role. *Your vision will not be rolled out until it has been taught.*

When the vision is talked about one on one and explained to volunteers and leaders, then ultimately we will see the vision fulfilled. Until they can explore the vision and the direction of the church, there will be a lack of

Don't let the fear of the time it will take to accomplish something stand in the way of doing it.

clarity. Jesus communicated to the large group, broke into small groups to allow the teaching to sink in and allow the dialogue to become part of them. Too often we want to rescue volunteers and leaders and give answers, but looking at Jesus' teaching, questions were answered with questions or parables. Having questions helps to deepen our walk with God as leaders, and finding solutions themselves helps to deepen the faith of your volunteers.

HOW TO PULL LEADERSHIP OUT OF PEOPLE

Remain silent. It is important for a leader to know when to remain silent, even if you have the solution. Giving people answers does not duplicate leaders as much as asking the questions to help them come up with the answers they are looking for on their own.

There is a thought process involved in placing the right people in the right seat of leadership. Or, it is possible that the right people can also be put in the wrong seat. What you want to avoid is the wrong *person*. Choosing a servant who isn't ready for leadership will end up causing problems for themselves, for you and for the church—regardless what seat you offer.

You need to constantly evaluate whether you are in the right or wrong seat *yourself*, as well as the people you are leading! Is the ministry moving forward and moving smoothly? If not, then you need to love the volunteers and move them through the change required for movement to happen. We need to be able to shift people to a place where their gifts can best be used. You don't want to allow a disgruntled volunteer to stay in a position and be a virus to the organization, multiplying negativity. Regardless of the circumstances and how you deal with them, you need to serve with the right attitude.

> *"Your attitude must be like my own, for I, the Messiah, did not come to be served, but to serve."*
> Matthew 20:28 (LB)

Choosing the right people is critical. Christ had lots of choices, but he saw something in each one of his disciples that showed him that they could do what He was doing.

You need to trust people you are training to do what you are doing. If you don't trust that they can do it, you probably haven't chosen the right people. If that's the case, then everyone will be frustrated and you will end up with twice the work to do.

A Jewish rabbi took time with his students. He heard their thoughts, their philosophies and their perspectives. He witnessed their ability to solve problems and how they dealt with overload. He listened and watched for characteristics in his students that resembled his own. If he thought, "That's how I would do it," he might believe that this particular student was the right one to duplicate him. If instead he thought, "Oh that's NOT how I would have done it..." then he would tell the student that he would be better off engaging in the family trade.

A rabbi's disciple was learning to duplicate what the rabbi did. After he learned how to do what the rabbi modeled, he would then became a rabbi. With time and experience, he would adapt what he had learned to make it his own way of doing things—slightly different, but building on what he had learned from his teacher. Until he became a rabbi himself, he fell under the authority of his teacher, taking what he was taught and doing it. Only when he had "done" it and become a rabbi in his own right would he change it.

It's important to know whether a person is fit for the work. As a leader, you should find fulfillment in pouring yourself into others. The rabbi would take the time to watch his student grow up, move through the process of becoming fit for discipleship, learning the Torah, the Old Testament, theology, watching him and listening for spiritual growth and leadership ability.

Sometimes a leader makes a mistake in the interest of time. He or she sees a need and decides to fill it without taking the time to invest in the person they are leading, choosing the wrong person because the leader didn't take the time to understand the depth of that person's ability, shape or character.

If you skip steps along the way, like getting to know the person you are teaching in the interest of expedience, then you will probably become angry with the person and you will both fail. It is the leader's responsibility to take the time to get to know the person and make sure they are in the right place, with the right content in developing competency and are experienced in making decisions that are required.

I can tell or I can show. I can send an email or model a behavior. Leadership is more than email directions without a model. I have told the traffic ministry volunteers about praying for the cars as they whiz by our campus, but when I did it with them, it communicated more clearly. Combining words with a model is more likely to achieve the action you are looking for. Leaders of others actually LEAD.

STORY: *Once I chose a small group leader to become a part of my team by bringing him into leadership, intending to give him ownership and a part of decision making. His position was overseeing the small group coaches who supervised small group leaders. The man went power-crazy! He felt he had much more knowledge than the small group coaches and lorded it over them. He needed to be removed from his seat of leadership.*

It was a great learning experience. When people with problems are given ownership with the intent of solving those problems, sometimes there are more problems that arise, especially if the person is in a position that is not aligned with their gifting. If they ARE aligned with their gifts, there can be success. If not, then you need to find ways to challenge them, occupy their time and not cause problems. Most people are miserable if they are not spending at least 80% of their time within their strength zone.

THINK ABOUT IT: *Every leader and volunteer needs to be asked, "Are you bored?" Is there something else you would rather be doing that would be more challenging? Is it time to change? If you do that when a volunteer seems* *to be meddling or fermenting discontent, the next time that person is intruding in another person's ministry, the conversation can move ahead. " It sounds like you are interested in doing something else." Every leader, every volunteer should ask, "Am I in the right seat?"*

ENJOY THE JOURNEY

This is the season to enjoy the journey. Every season is. In the fall you enjoy watching leaves change colors and then shower the streets and your yard with leaves. In the winter there is the rhythm of the falling rain or watching the snow fill your yard, covering your bushes and trees with a fluffy, white blanket. In the spring the birds return, flowers emerge from their dormancy and fresh new life is everywhere. Summer warms the earth, and blossoms become delicious fruit. You can enjoy the seasons and all the experiences of each new opportunity, or you can hate the fall because of all the leaves you have to pick up. You can hate winter because of the floods that the rain brings or the snow you have to shovel. You can hate the spring because of the anoying allergies and noisy birds, and despair in the summer because it's hot, full of mosquitos and the fruit that drops all over the ground!

Ministry is like that. You can enjoy the journey of getting stronger, the relationships you have, the process of building what's needed into lives, and how God seems to be using you and doing things through you. We all need to celebrate what IS happening. We need to do ministry like Abel.

> *When they grew up, Abel became a shepherd, while Cain cultivated the ground. When it was time for the harvest, Cain presented some of his crops as a gift to the Lord. Abel also brought a gift—the best of the firstborn lambs from his flock. The Lord accepted Abel and his gift, but he did not accept Cain and his gift. This made Cain very angry, and he looked dejected. 'Why are you so angry?' the Lord asked Cain. 'Why do you look so dejected? You will be accepted if you do what is right, then watch out! Sin is crouching at the door, eager to control you. But you must subdue it and be its master.' One day Cain suggested to his brother, 'Let's go out into the fields.' And while they were in the field, Cain attacked his brother, Abel, and killed him.* Genesis 4:2-8 (NLT)

Both men had made an offering to God. Abel's was accepted, but Cain's was not. Their lives and attitudes can be compared to serving in two ways: in the spirit of Abel or the spirit of Cain. Both men worked hard, used their gifts, made an offering to God. The difference between them was their attitude in making and presenting the offering. Cain became bitter and may have been thinking, "why do this anymore? I'm tired, frustrated, burned out. Shouldn't someone else be doing this? Is this even making a difference?" Abel had a good attitude toward giving and toward God who breathed life into him. He had a song in his heart, and his first priority and goal was to honor God. He offered his best. Cain, however, was unwilling to adjust to God's suggestion and became more bitter, ungrateful and jealous. When he killed Abel he was enraged and unconnected with his purpose to honor God with his life.

We have a choice as leaders to serve with a spirit of Abel or the spirit of Cain: to enjoy the seasons or hate the seasons. We can enjoy the process of life or be bitter through the process of life.

Comparison for the sake of education may be useful, but it can also build up pride in your heart because you feel you are doing more or a better job. When you live in the world of comparison, it can also deflate you and cause you to become discouraged because you think *someone else* is doing a better job or more than you. When you are comparing, you never have the time to enjoy the journey. If you can't enjoy today, then you will probably not enjoy where you are tomorrow.

If you are reading this and your response is, "Yes, but..." then you've just identified yourself as someone who is not enjoying the journey. It's time to learn contentment and enjoy today. If tomorrow is better than today, then GREAT. The process of enjoying the journey is enjoying today, regardless of what tomorrow holds. It's all a matter of heart.

> *"But you are not like that, for you are a chosen people. You are royal priests, a holy nation, God's very own possession. As a result, you can show others the goodness of God, for he called you out of the darkness into his wonderful light."* 1 Peter 2:9 (NLT)

BREATHE

I had never really realized how much God focused on breathing throughout the Bible—until now. Breathing was not only what God chose to give humans life, it was also what he chose to remind us of our creator.

> *"The LORD God took a handful of soil and made a man. God breathed life into the man, and the man started breathing."* Genesis 2:7 (CEV)

God took something that was dead: inert earth that had no life, no power to communicate, think or feel and pressed it into a human shape. But that alone wasn't enough for the person to live. Even though it was molded by God and created in God's image, nothing took place until he breathed into the formed soil. Once God breathed into this sand castle of a human being, at that moment the sand castle was no longer an image but a living being. It was in that moment of God's breath that life began for mankind.

I have never paid attention to the number of breaths I take in a minute, hour, or day. I sometimes check the number of times my heart beats in a minute or how many times it beats while I am exercising but I seldom notice the quantity of air running in and out of my body.

Putting it into perspective, on average, an individual inhales and exhales about fifteen times in a minute. That is 900 breaths per hour, and about 21, 600 breaths per day! Of course there is a lot that can change that number. For example, your health condition determines the number of respirations you have in a day. Marathon runners obviously take fewer breaths a day than the rest of us non-marathon runners.

God could have created us to breathe less frequently, but for some reason he chose to create us in such a way that we would need to take thousands of breaths per day. My mind always wants to ask simple questions like "Why God?"—"Why would you want me to take that many breaths a day?"—"What are you teaching me about breathing?—What is it that I can learn from what I have been thinking about, and now writing and reading about?"

Who has time to stop and pay attention to their breathing? Not me! How many of us in leadership ever stop being busy long enough to listen to the rhythm and sound of our breathing? I think there is more to breathing than I ever imagined.

> *"'Now go to the king! I am sending you to lead my people out of his country.' But Moses said, 'Who am I to go to the king and lead your people out of Egypt?' God replied, 'I will be with you. And you will know that I am the one who sent you, when you worship me on this mountain after you have led my people out of Egypt.' Moses answered, 'I will tell the people of Israel that the God their ancestors worshiped has sent me to them. But what should I say, if they ask me your name?' God said to Moses: 'I am the eternal God. So tell them that the LORD, whose name is "I Am," has sent you. This is my name forever, and it is the name that people must use from now on.'"*
>
> Exodus 3:10-15 (CEV)

So many times I have read these Scriptures and focused on God's mission for Moses or his desire to free his people from Egypt, or the lessons for Moses as he learned to rely on God's power instead of his own, or the revelation of the name of God. Whenever I focused on verse fifteen concerning the name of God I have always gravitated towards the "...I AM" part and almost every time ignored the "...LORD" part. But now, looking at the LORD part of verse fifteen, I notice that the LORD is the emphasis to God's name "I AM." I looked up how often the word LORD appears in the Bible and although translations vary it is safe to say that it appears more than 6,000 times. Once again my mind poses the question: "God why would LORD appear more than 6,000 times in the Bible?" Just like my previous question, "God why would you want me to breathe more than 21, 600 times a day?"

In the Old Testament's original Hebrew, the word LORD is actually spelled as the letters, "YHVH." Ancient rabbis didn't believe these letters were pronounced as an actual word because when you pronounce these letters they sound like breathing. Try it: Yod, Hey, Vav, Hey, Yod, Hey, Vav, Hey. Could the name of God be the sound of breathing? Or, think about it: if God is LORD and LORD is YHVH (breathing) then the act of breathing is saying the name of God 21,600 times a day!

This makes sense of why the sand castle human was empty until God placed himself, his breath, into the lifeless form to give it life.

What happens when you stop the busyness of your life and take time to be aware of the rhythm of your breathing, listening to your breath coming in and out of your body? If you focus on the breaths and not on what's on your mind you will be, in effect, saying God's name over and over again. Yod, hey, Vav, Hey—and as you do this over and over, you begin to slow down your breathing, begin to slow down your day, begin to let go of your worries, stress, exhaustion and begin to REST. Who would have thought that focusing on God 21,600 times a day would give you passion, energy, and REST?

Breathing during ministry isn't simply so you can have rest during ministry, breathing during ministry is so you can stay

Breathing during ministry isn't simply so you can have rest during ministry, it is so you can stay focused on God.

focused on God—so that God can be present in every breath you take. As you love, minister, meet needs, work, build relationships, invite, connect, invest, recruit, equip and duplicate, God isn't an ignored moment but a present reality. With every breath—

and as you go about pouring your life into people, saying words like, "Hi, nice to meet you," "Great seeing you today," "Glad to meet you," "Thank you for being here," "Good morning," "How are you?"—you can be aware of the presence of God. Those words you speak require you to breathe and to speak the word, "Lord" as you create a relational connection or invest further into someone else's life.

It is one thing to have oxygen around you, it is another to have oxygen *in* you. Every day you swim in a ocean of oxygen but that means nothing if oxygen isn't going in and out of your lungs. God has breathed life into us, and it is impossible to live without breathing the name of God. Yet so many people have used the name of God to say, "I no longer want to invest my life for God." For example:

"I'm burned out of ministry" requires you breathe God's name at least seven times that you no longer want to minister for God.

"I'm tired of serving" is equivalnt to at least four times that you have to breathe "LORD" to say you no longer want to serve.

REST

> *"On the sixth day God completed all the work that he had done, and on the seventh day God rested from all the work that he had done."* Genesis 2:2 (CEB)

"...God rested..." I doubt it was because God was tired or because he needed it. The reality was that WE need to know how important rest is. It is so important that God himself took time to show us rest.

> *"So you see that a Sabbath rest is left open for God's people. The one who entered God's rest also rested from his works, just as God rested from his own. Therefore, let's make every effort to enter that rest so that no one will fall by following the same example of disobedience."* Hebrews 4:9-11 (CEB)

God never intended for us to be burned out, tired or exhausted. He intended for us to rely on Him more than relying on ourselves. He intended for you and I to BREATHE, rest and have energy and passion. He intended for us to breathe the name of God at least 21,600 times a day as we partner with Him to love and be in relationship with others. May you be reminded of your creator as you learn to BREATHE in ministry.

No stranger to understanding the value of teams, Moses was raised in a home where the family was a team, able to do far more together than individually, alone.

That was a good beginning. Moses Camacho has served in leadership positions from serving as a youth pastor in a tiny church in Corona, California to leading a regional campus for Saddleback Church in Huntington Beach.

Beginning as a volunteer in youth ministry, he learned the value of teams as God led him into more responsibility, greater challenges, successes, failures and exhaustion.

Through experience, he has learned to maintain his passion, to BREATHE and stretch his vision through team relationships and to value collaboration far above individual achievement.

Married to Jill Camacho and father to three energetic little boys, Caleb, Caden and Ezra, Moses calls family his "number one team."

Moses Camacho
Regional Pastor
Saddleback Huntington Beach

CPSIA information can be obtained at www.ICGtesting.com
Printed in the USA
LVOW01s0035180713

343461LV00012B/211/P

9 780988 490406